STAR QUALTY EXPERIENCE

The Hotelier's Guide to Creating
Memorable Guest Journeys

MONICA OR

RETHINK PRESS

First published in Great Britain 2016
by Rethink Press (www.rethinkpress.com)

STAR QUALITY EXPERIENCE

The Hotelier's Guide to Creating Memorable Guest Journeys

WHAT OTHERS ARE SAYING ABOUT THE BOOK

Monica Or's book is exhilarating, inspiring and covers every aspect of delivering a 'Star Quality Experience'. I have no hesitation recommending this book to students studying hotel management, hoteliers progressing their careers, and to experienced hoteliers wishing to consistently exceed the expectations of their guests by adding unique value.

Monica presents her book in seven easy to follow steps that if practised will create a memorable customer journey. The relationship and trust you develop with your customer is unique to you and can't be copied and is the key to the success of your business. We live in an age when at the click of a button customers can communicate a good or bad experience to thousands.

Monica explains how you can grow your business by reputation and good word of mouth, which far exceeds any benefits derived from advertising. In a fast changing world, listening and getting closer to your customers has never been more important. This timely book will inspire you to develop a strategy that will create a consistent star quality experience.

Harry Murray MBE MI FIH
– Chairman, Lucknam Park Hotel & Spa

As in her previous book Star Quality Hospitality – The Key to a Successful Hospitality Business, *Monica manages to explain the complex world of hotels in a very straightforward manner. I am sure that this will continue to inspire and educate more people to come into our fantastic industry!*

Andrew Thomson
– General Manager, The Halkin by COMO

I found Monica's book a delight to read as it was interesting and engaging. The exercises were helpful in honing one's thoughts into a constructive list of actions and processes. It was interesting reading about the opinions of others in the industry and how Monica was able to bring them all together in a cohesive manner. Well done, Monica! I look forward to the next one.

Alexandra Tollman
– Director of Sales, Red Carnation Hotels

This book gives you a lot of tips and support into how you can create a better experience for your guests. Expectations are constantly increasing by the demands we set ourselves. You will find quotes of respected hospitality professionals on how they create special moments in various ways.

It is a great opportunity to look at your own business and ask yourself some key questions about the business you work in, or use this book as a training tool for your teams. It has helped me to check if we are doing the things we should be doing! Monica also talks about how your business can be perceived online through your website and social media, points which are very valid in the modern age.

Roy Sommer
– Hotel Manager, Courthouse Hotel London

A great insight of how to create memorable guest experiences using a variety of different platforms, making it accessible to operators at all levels of the business. The exercises, case studies and top tips make this book a tool that can be used by any hospitality professional to ensure their guests have a stay to remember.

Adam Rowledge FIH
– General Manager, Georgian House

I think this is absolutely relevant to our sector of the industry and is a great tool for independent hoteliers. I love the 7 Rs model, and will be using the book as an excellent training tool for my managers. I found the 'true life' examples very interesting and the tips excellent. Even though I have been in the hotel management trade over thirty years, there was plenty within the pages of the book I would draw upon for resources.

Jason Hilton
– Owner, De Rougemont Manor

Following on from her first book on how to maintain a successful hospitality business, Monica moves on to help those in the industry with insights on the current trends to improving engagement with guests, delivering tips to create holistic customer focused strategies. Clear and concise for both those in the industry and those who want to be.

Steven McGovern
– Director of Sales and Marketing,
The Stafford London

Star Quality Experience *comes across as a unique book that in a direct and efficient language welcomes the reader into the dynamic and international world of hospitality. Monica Or decodes in an accessible and clear writing style the secrets of a perfect customer experience. Furthermore, thanks to the support and active participation of well-known professionals from the hospitality sector, priceless examples of the know-how for different situations are well portrayed in front of the reader. Customer needs mirror societal trends. The former are likely to change as fast as you could possibly expect from a world that nowadays does not sleep overnight anymore.*

Monica's book is full of useful resources that commit the reader by promoting active reading and learning. Additionally, she has designed and written each chapter using a constructive and effective learning method. Therefore, when the reader reaches the end of the book, a real strategy is magically discovered and may be easily and efficiently put into practice. Star Quality Experience *supports the reader in creating a unique system for both short and long term ROI, the latter being crucial to understand and measure if the strategies adopted may be considered successful.*

Monica Or has written a definitive book that comes across as an important guideline to follow in today's competitive hospitality and tourism industry.

Francesco Antonazzo
– Room Service Manager, South Place Hotel

The 7 Rs Model created by Monica is a valuable tool for all hospitality students to understand and learn to apply whilst on their journey to become hoteliers of the future – this book should be required reading for all hospitality management students.

Kelly Vadukar
– Marketing and Guest Experience Specialist,
Glion Institute of Higher Education

This book is a brilliant tool that can be referenced time and time again, demonstrating a number of top tips and approaches to achieving really fantastic hospitality. Detailing real-life scenarios that hoteliers can relate to, this easy-to-follow guide covers every aspect of the customer journey, and what you can do to improve it at every step. The bite-size chapters mean readers can dip in and out easily and use it as a regular training source to brush up on skills or learn something for the first time.

I was hugely impressed with the level of detail contained in the book and defy anybody not to put it down feeling inspired!

Zoe Monk
– Editor, Boutique Hotelier

CONTENTS

FOREWORD

There's an old saying in our business that 'hospitality is the art of making your guests feel at home... when you wish they were'. Few hoteliers would subscribe to that today because they need as many guests as possible to meet their vast operating costs. Failures abound in this highly competitive field so it behoves the novice to learn all they can about creating great guest experiences without overspending.

During my years in hospitality it has become clear that hoteliers tend to survive the economic roller coaster by being either the cheapest or the best of their kind. Both are incredibly hard to achieve, and yet we are blessed with hundreds of examples in Britain of people who manage to delight their guests day after day while making a decent profit into the bargain. Such people are heroes, in my estimation, although the best of them remain modest about their success.

Anyone who reads this book will quickly see that making your customer feel special requires attention to thousands of details. It explains how the 'journey' actually starts long before she gets in the car and ends long after she has returned home – it covers the search and booking process all the way through to the decision whether or not to visit again, not forgetting of course the actual stay in between.

Monica Or is a keen observer of independent hotels and has advised many in her professional life as a consultant. You will not be surprised, therefore, to find within these pages a good deal of common sense that anyone working in hotels can apply to their own role, whether in management, marketing or front of house. But there are also secrets to putting a smile on the guest's face that cost nothing – these she describes as 'random acts of kindness' – which create that sense of generosity which everyone appreciates and which can turn first timers into precious repeat guests.

Underpinning all of this is learning how to relate to guests through conversation. For all the digital advances we now benefit from, human contact remains key to everything and there is an interesting section on communicating effectively. It is worth noting that around half of all hotel bookings are still made by telephone, even when the initial search took place online, and that postal campaigns can still trump email ones in certain circumstances.

Great hoteliers make it look easy, don't they? They appear to have limitless funds to throw at their properties and copious smiling staff to take care of every little detail. How very decep-tive this can be. Like show business, the art of hospitality is a marriage of sparkling performances on stage with sheer hard work in far from glamorous conditions behind the scenes.

I have been lucky enough to become acquainted with dozens of great hoteliers who need little advice on how to deliver a 'star quality experience'. Ironically, they are the very people most likely to buy this book because the greatest exponents of hospitality, by nature, never want to stop learning.

Peter Hancock FIH MI
– Chief Executive, Pride of Britain Hotels

Peter Hancock has spent almost forty years in the hospitality industry and is currently Chief Executive of Pride of Britain Hotels. He is also a popular speaker at dinners, lunches and conferences where his clarity of voice, good timekeeping and wit add to the pleasure of these occasions. Discover more: www.peterhancock.org.uk

INTRODUCTION

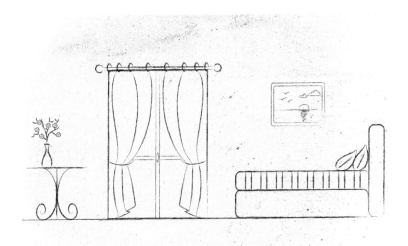

It has been said that a picture paints a thousand words and the best way to capture a memory is by taking photos. In this day and age these photos are no longer just kept in dusty photo albums but are shared globally online thanks to social media. How many times have you had your guests take photos of your bedrooms or your food and instantly post them on Facebook, Twitter or Instagram? This should be an everyday occurrence, and I should know because I am one of those guests who does it all the time. If it is really spectacular I may even make a short video and blog about my experience, or write a review online.

These days our guests are very snap happy and will post up almost anything on social media. So you need to ensure that the photos they take of your hotel show your business in its best light. Having a photo of a bland looking bedroom (like the one illustrated in the cartoons in this book) will not do your hotel any favours. The photos that you want your guests to share have to show what a great experience your hotel can offer.

The best form of advertising is carried out by word of mouth, and thanks to technology this can be carried far and wide. For your business to be successful not only do you want people to be talking about it for all the right reasons, but you want them to be shouting from the rooftops what an amazing experience they had while staying with you... preferably on review sites such as TripAdvisor because, love it or loathe it, this is the main point of call for potential guests to find out more about your property. It is a proven fact that customers trust reviews written by other customers about products they have tried, tested and bought.

The challenge for you as an independent hotelier is to work out how to get your guest to come back time and again, and each time give them something a little different from the last time they stayed with you. We all know we have to exceed our guest expectations, but how can this be sustainable so it does not become contrived? What we need to remember is that each guest is unique and so all of your guests will have a different experience with you. All you have to work out is how to make it memorable for that individual.

Think back to the last time you stayed in a hotel. It may have been for a night, a week or maybe longer. What do you actually remember about that stay? Regardless of the length of time of your stay, in order for you to get to the hotel you would have gone on a journey, and that journey would have continued throughout the whole of your stay until you got back home. This book is going to look at how hoteliers can make the journey more complete for their guests by turning it from a routine transaction into a memorable experience. For the independent hotelier it is vital, now more than ever, that you step up your game and deliver what your guests expect. There is always another hotel down the road that they will take their custom to if they are not satisfied.

According to research carried out by BDO (2014), the Top 20 Hotel Companies by number of rooms in the UK show how the budget sector is prevalent. Whitbread, owner of the Premier Inn brand, and Travelodge combined account for over 48% of the total hotels within the Top 20 list. Independent hotels will never make it on a list like this because the branded chains have too many properties for them to compete with. In 2015 there were forty-five planned hotel openings for Premier Inn and Travelodge across the UK alone. By the very nature of being independent, though, you have the advantage over these companies in the products and service you have to offer to your guests.

While researching for this book I wanted to find out what hoteliers are currently doing for their guests. I interviewed numerous leading hospitality professionals from the luxury hotel sector to find out their take on creating a star quality experience for their guests. I have included their insights to illustrate a simple model that I have designed. You can use this to ensure that whenever you have a guest stay at your hotel, or dine in your restaurant, they are taken on a memorable guest journey. Their journey will be individualised and personalised through the interactions they have with the hospitality professionals they meet along the way. It will not cost you a fortune to use these principles in your own hotel, although it could cost you through lost revenue if you do not.

This book is the follow-up to my first book, *Star Quality Hospitality – The Key to a Successful Hospitality Business*, which looked at the overall business structure, process and procedures that have to be in place to run a successful hotel or restaurant, taking into account who your customers are. It looks at your supplier relationship, how you develop your staff and how you look after your guests. I am now taking this further and concentrating on what you, the hotelier, have to do to ensure your guest books with you, stays with you, comes back and recommends you.

The model I have created is the '7 Rs To Creating Memorable Guest Journeys':

Resources

This first section will look at the *resources* you have available for your guest to find you. This means the presence of your website, how responsive it is and how easy it is for your guests to book with you online. Can your guest book with you directly or do they get diverted through to an online travel agent (OTA) which is costing you a small fortune? When researching, potential guests will always read your TripAdvisor reviews – what are they saying about you?

Response

The second R is all about your *response*. Here we will look at what happens pre-arrival and on arrival to ensure every guest receives a warm welcome.

Rapport

The third R is about how you build *rapport* with your guests. This looks at the importance of your service levels and how you can use them to anticipate your guests' needs; how awareness and attention to detail are key prompts for you.

Refine

The fourth R is all about how to *refine* your service – how the use of guest profiles can assist you to personalise a guest's stay. This is what will make your guest journey a success rather than just a stopping point, but none of this is of any use if it is not communicated clearly with the whole of your team.

Reviews

The fifth R is all about the goodbye and what happens afterwards. How do you get your guest to *review* their stay with you because you left a lasting impression that they want to share?

Retain

Having gone to all the trouble of looking after your guest, you want to *retain* them. So this sixth section looks at tips on how to let your guest know you are still thinking about them even though they are not currently staying with you.

Return

The final R is all about what to do when your guest *returns*. It costs five times more to attract a new guest than to keep an existing guest, so it makes sense to have as much repeat business as possible.

Throughout this book there are examples from hoteliers I have interviewed, demonstrating what they have done to ensure they are giving a star quality experience in order to create memorable guest journeys. So to learn some top tips and ways to enhance your guest experience, which can be implemented easily into your hotel, read on…

CREATING A
STAR QUALITY EXPERIENCE

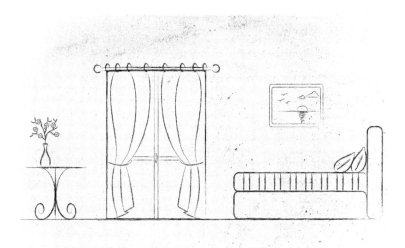

Star Quality

What do we mean by a Star Quality Experience?

When we talk about having a 'Star Quality Experience', we
want to create an experience for our guests which will make
them feel important and give them the quality of product
and service they deserve.

Each individual guest you serve will have their own perception of what it feels like for them to be treated like a star. It may be they want the full pamper treatment and want to be totally fussed over, and when they make an entrance everyone knows they have made an entrance. Or it could be that they want a seamless service where everything is done for them without them having to think about it, and it is the discretion of your staff that gives them an air of importance. Their perception of quality will also vary, from wanting the best Egyptian cotton sheets on their beds with no expense spared to having a meal that tastes delicious but does not break the bank for them.

When it comes to creating an experience for your guests, this is what tends to happen: some hotels will focus on their product, using the most expensive and exclusive furnishings, having the most up to date technology so guests can self-check-in and bedrooms with motion detectors that will operate the lighting and electronics in the room. Others will focus on their service standards, ensuring that every guest is treated as an individual and their needs are met and expectations exceeded. However, you cannot have one without the other because:

Product + Service = Experience

What you need to do is to create a star quality experience for your guests. These experiences will be individual to that guest, and because of this they will become a lasting memory for them.

You may not be running a luxury five star hotel with the most up to date technology or be able to afford to have designer furnishings. The style of your hotel and the ambience you generate are what will help to create your experience, and the same principles can still be applied in a small guest house or bed and breakfast. Your product does not have to be the most luxurious, although it does have to be clean, up to date and presentable. Delivering a five star service is not only for five star hotels. Regardless of your rating, your service should always be at its best, and the delivery of this service all comes down to how personable and courteous you are.

In my first book *Star Quality Hospitality – The Key to a Successful Hospitality Business* I explain where the word 'hospitality' comes from. In the olden days pineapples were impaled on the front gate to welcome visitors, and due to this history the universal symbol for hospitality is a pineapple to represent people being made welcome. Although this is now recognised worldwide, these days there is no need for the pineapple, but there is still a need to be hospitable. Sometimes we forget how to do this, which shows in our service delivery.

When I interviewed hoteliers for this book I asked them what their definition of customer service was, and one hotelier explained this in a way which really shows how to make the difference.

Rowledge (2015) said, 'Service and hospitality are different. "Service" is a process of how to do things efficiently, whereas "hospitality" is about feelings and engaging with your guest.' This is what tends to be lacking when you enter a property that is just service focused. We are in the service industry, but at times our service becomes robotic and the warmth is often missing. At times we seem to forget that we are also in the hospitality industry, and being hospitable is why we open the doors of our hotel in the first place.

Another issue that happens when we run our hotels is that we think we know who our guests are, but do we really? When I ask this question of my clients, the majority answer, 'Corporate and leisure', but what does that actually mean for your hotel?

When I interviewed my hoteliers, the majority of them were able to describe in great detail who their customers are – their backgrounds, the companies they work for – and from this I could get a clear picture of whom they were accommodating. To be able to understand what your guests really want from your business, you have to get to know them, and to do that you have to ask them.

Exercise – How well do you know your guests?

Think about one of your regular guests and write down ten things you know about them.

1

2

3

4

5

6

7

8

9

10

Were you able to come up with ten things? If you really know your guests, the sort of things you may have written down would include name, company they work for, their job, favourite food, favourite drink, any allergies, specific table they like in the restaurant, their birthday, names of family members, hobbies, pets, where they went on holiday – the list can go on. In order to find this information out you have to talk to your guests and get to know them. The more you talk to them, the more they will tell you. People like talking about themselves.

Once you get to know your guests, you can then simply ask them what it is that they like about your hotel. Why did they choose to stay with you? What are you doing that makes them come back again and again? You may be surprised with the answers you get.

The guest journey

When a customer chooses to stay at your hotel they will go on a journey. Throughout this journey they will come upon many opportunities for what Carlzon (2001) refers to as 'moments of truth'. He believed that it is important for organisations to identify every point of contact that customers may have with that organisation by phone, email, reading about it or any other way. Each contact that they have with your business, or anyone who is connected with your business, provides an opportunity to form an opinion about your company. This point of contact is critical for you as it is at this point that your customer will decide whether or not they wish to do business with you.

Carlzon (2001) relays a story about a gentleman called Rudy Peterson who was staying at a hotel in Stockholm. One day he had to fly to Copenhagen for a day trip. When he arrived at the airport he realised that he had left his passport in his hotel room. He thought that when he got to the check-in desk he would be turned away.

He was pleasantly surprised by the response he got. The

ticket agent gave him his boarding card and issued him a temporary ticket. She then asked him where he was staying and where he had left his passport and told him not to worry as she would arrange for it to be collected from the hotel and delivered to the airport. This was all duly done in good time for Mr Peterson to make his flight.

This is a moment of truth example that SAS Airlines pride themselves on, and just one of numerous moments of truth carried out by their staff. Their customers do not talk about the airline in terms of their planes but with regards to the experiences their staff provide them.

Exercise – moments of truth (MOT)

Imagine you are a customer who would stay in your hotel, and think through the different moment of truth opportunities you will have. Make a note of every single time you would contact the hotel or a member of staff throughout your customer journey.

MOT 1

MOT 2

MOT 3

MOT 4

MOT 5

MOT 6

MOT 7

MOT 8

MOT 9

MOT 10

The number of moment of truth opportunities you come up with will depend on your hotel and the facilities you have, as well as the type of customer you serve. As we have already mentioned, every customer is individual, so their journeys will be unique to them.

The example below shows what could be the start of your

guest journey where your customer will come across various moments of truth. If not handled correctly, these could result in lost opportunities:

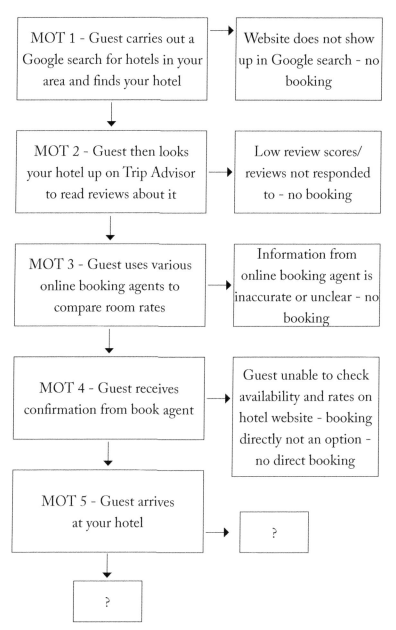

The above example only shows the very beginning of our guest journey, but it can be seen that at every moment of truth point there could be a lost opportunity. How this guest journey will evolve will all depend on who the guest meets and interacts with along the way. More than likely while the guests are in your hotel, it will be your staff who will either create moments of truth for them or lose the opportunity to connect and make a lasting impression.

Take another look at the above example – what is really happening here? The guest is in control of their actions – they are making the decision whether or not to continue their journey with you. What you have to do is to ensure that for every step of their journey there is no turning back. The longer you keep them on their journey and create moments of truth for them, the more loyal your guest will become.

We have introduced what we mean by a star quality experience, and how by being hospitable we can create moments of truth to connect with our guests. It is now time to take this one step further and implement the 7 Rs of creating memorable guest journeys.

RESOURCES – MAKE IT EASY FOR YOUR GUESTS TO FIND YOU

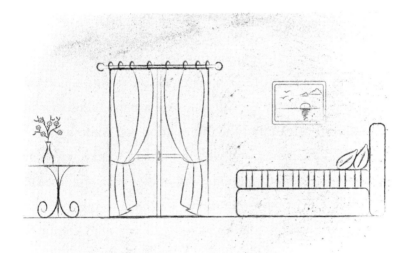

Hotel Search

This first section will look at the *Resources* you have available for your guest to find you – what your web presence is like, how easy it is for guests to book with you online, whether that be directly or via on online travel agent, and how to ensure you get glowing TripAdvisor reviews.

Your web presence

To be found online it is a given that you have a website, although your website should not be static. It should be a living, breathing representation of your hotel. Your website is the window that your guests will look through to find out more about what they will experience when they stay with you. Like a shop window, if your website stays the same and you have nothing new to show, then your customers will look elsewhere.

Imagine you are a guest wanting to book a weekend break away and you decide to do a search online to find a suitable hotel. The first hotel website you come across is slow to load and it is difficult to find the information you want. Some of the links do not work and you find it hard to navigate your way around. The information is out of date with reference to last year's Christmas promotions. You have to really search to find the hotel contact details to locate where it actually is, and there is no facility for you to check availability or book online.

The next website you go to loads very quickly with good quality photos and a short video that immediately gives you a feel of what the hotel is like. It is easy to navigate around with clear tabs, each page is consistent in its layout, and it has a location map which links through to Google so you can work out directions and find out how to get to the hotel. The bedrooms have clear images and descriptions so you can make a decision on the type of room you would like to book. You can check availability for the dates you want and the booking process is easy and secure. A couple of clicks later and you've made your booking.

Which website would you prefer to have?

When you are building your website, there are numerous things that need to be taken into consideration, and as technology progresses at an ever increasing speed it is important that you are able to keep up with it.

It is common knowledge that Google is the biggest search engine. What is not so well known is that the second biggest search engine is YouTube, so it makes sense to have a presence on both. The best way to do this is to have a video embedded in your website that is linked to YouTube.

According to Evans (2016), Cisco estimates that by 2019 video will make up 80% of consumer traffic. She suggests that a high quality video can introduce your guests not only to your property, but more importantly to the atmosphere, the staff, and the welcome that they can expect. By utilising your chefs, managers, and staff members in your video, you will be utilising the best ambassadors for your hotel that you can find. Show your guests what they can expect before they even arrive.

Evans (2016) goes on to advise that a video for today's market needs to be short. When a guest is researching a business, such as a hotel, a video of more than sixty to ninety seconds will never be watched to the end. As you only have a short time to sell in any one video, keep it to one topic – one video, one message. Sit down with your marketing team and decide what you want to focus on that is unique to your business – is it location; splendid rooms; the spa; the restaurant? Once you have decided, make it creative.

Does your website portray all of this? When was the last time you reviewed your own website?

Exercise – website review

Have a look at your website and check to see if it has the following:

- Easy navigation. As a general rule there should be no more than seven tabs as too many become overwhelming for the user. All links should work. The navigation bar should be on the same place on every page

- Clean and simple, easy to read and not too small font

- As few steps as possible to get to a 'call to action' button

- Up to date, relevant information, which is not too wordy, written in a way which highlights how you meet your customers' needs

---

- Good quality photos which are compressed correctly to speed up site loading

- A short video of between sixty and ninety seconds

- Social media links to attract followers and encourage engagement

- Contact information which includes full address with postcode, contact telephone number, email

- Enquiry form so queries can be dealt with immediately

- Online booking, as ideally you want your customers to book with you directly

- Easy and secure online payment process

- Option to translate information into another language. This can be done quite easily with Google Translate. Remember hospitality is an international concern, and hopefully you will be welcoming guests from all around the world.

Now for the more technical side, your website needs to:

- Be fully responsive. This means it can be viewed on any device, including smartphones and tablets. When the page is viewed, the size and layout is automatically adjusted for that device

- Have key search words and terms that will assist with Search Engine Optimisation (SEO). Ideally you want to be on the first page of a Google search organically

- Have Google analytics installed – you need to be able to monitor and track how your website is performing

- Have a Content Management System (CMS) that you, the user, can update, so any simple changes to your website you can do yourself.

To keep in the Google search rankings you will want to update your website on a regular basis. This could be done through updating promotional offers or menus, for example.

If there are any items above that you have not ticked off, or you are unsure of how to make the necessary changes, then you should ask your web developer. If you have built your website on a 'build your own' platform you may need to consider moving it and hiring a professional web developer to redesign it.

The following links may help you to decide if your website needs to be updated or redesigned:

Nibbler http://nibbler.silktide.com/. This is a free tool for testing websites. Just enter in your URL address and it will produce a report for you, scoring your website out of ten. The test will review five web pages, focusing on various aspects including accessibility, SEO, social media and technology. You should be looking for a score of eight or more.

Pingdom Website Speed Test http://tools.pingdom.com/fpt/. This tests how quickly your page loads. You should be aiming for a performance grade of 80–85% or above. The time it takes for your website to load is very important to your visitors. In fact, according to a survey, almost 50% of visitors expect a website to load in two seconds or fewer, and 40% of visitors abandon a website that takes more than three seconds to load.

Hoteliers tend to think that everything centres around their website and this is the first place their potential guests go to, but you need to remember that your website is just one tool to get guests to book with you. In order to find your website in the first place, your potential guests will be relying heavily on Google searches. This means that your SEO has to be strong on the key words you use to ensure you are on page one of these organic searches.

When your potential guest uses Google as their first point of call, their search will be along the lines of hotel + destination. They will look at reviews and social media next before going to online travel agents to compare prices, and then they will look at your hotel's website before deciding whether or not to book with you. Knowing how your potential guest thinks when they are planning their stay with you will help you to work out where you need to have a presence online.

A word about using social media

Whether or not you use social media should be a business choice rather than a personal choice. The main reason for social media is to grow an online community that you can engage with. It can be time consuming, so unless you are willing to post regularly and update your community on what you are doing, then it may be best to stay clear. It also depends on your customer base. If they are avid users of social media then you should have a presence.

When used correctly, social media can be a great way to gain referrals through word of mouth and to spread your message far and wide.

According to a survey conducted by Visit Britain (2015):

- Facebook was the main go-to source for respondents in all stages of the holiday making process, especially those who visited Britain

- Twitter was most used for seeking suggestions and advice

- Instagram was used by people who wanted to plan their trip or share experiences.

So let's look at how to utilise these popular platforms:

Facebook https://www.facebook.com/ – where you can set up an organisation page. You first need to have a personal account with Facebook, and once this has been set up you can create your organisation page for your business. You then post updates, which could include photos, videos and promotions for your hotel.

Ideally you want to be sharing news about your hotel rather than constantly pushing sales promotions as you want to create interest and loyalty. The 80/20 rule is that 80% of the time you post about local interests and facts to engage your audience, and 20% of the time your posts are about your hotel promotions.

You can create brand awareness of your business through your fan base as people 'like' your page. Potential customers can find out more about your hotel through this page so always include a direct link to your website. To get the most out of using your Facebook organisation page, you may want to consider using targeted Facebook advertising as well. These adverts will only appear to people on Facebook who have shown an interest in your product and services.

Twitter https://twitter.com/ – which can be set up under your hotel name. This is currently used to post short updates of no more than 140 characters so you need to be succinct in your messages. When using Twitter there are certain jargon, tips and tricks you need to be aware of:

- Twitter handle – this is your username which will start with @, so your Twitter handle might be @hotelname

- Tweet – this is a 140 character message

- Retweet – abbreviated as RT, this will share a message from another user

- Feed – the stream of tweets you will get on your homepage which is made up of updates from the users you follow

- Mention – a way to mention another user is to use their Twitter handle in your tweet, for example @hotelguest

- Direct message, abbreviated to DM – a private message from one user to another. You can only direct message users who follow you

- Hashtag – #, a symbol used as a discovery tool to find specific words.

As you only have 140 characters you may want to shorten a URL link that you post in your message. You can do this by using tools such as Tiny URL http://tinyurl.com/ where you paste in the full URL and this tool will shorten it for you. You can then use the shortened version in your tweet. If you really cannot manage only 140 characters then you can also use www.twitlonger.com or www.longertweets.com to write a longer post. These applications will create a URL link to your full post.

To tell you more about using Twitter, Simply Business has put together a very easy to use guide:

http://www.simplybusiness.co.uk/microsites/twitter-for-small-businesses/

Instagram https://business.instagram.com/ – uses visual storytelling where you can capture moments such as an image of your hotel in the snow, a sunset, or a romantic dinner. Create your moments, capture them in photos or video and share them on this platform. Let the images speak for themselves.

Instagram combines the two most powerful aspects of social media – imagery and sharing – and is particularly popular with hotel guests, foodies and travellers. You may have heard of the term 'food porn'. This is when the dishes you create look so tantalising that your guest wants to take a photo and share it with the world. Great photos grab attention, convey a sense of place, inspire people to eat, travel, and don't require translation.

I would also add another platform, **Google+ for Business** https://plus.google.com/, as using anything related to Google always helps with your search engine rankings. Google+ is slightly different to other social media platforms in that you can select whom you share your posts with. You can have separate circles if you want to share some posts with certain individuals, or you could post publically which means anyone can see them. Google+ for Business will also provide you with a Google Map to show where your business is located – your customers can review your business here too – and you will be linked to a host of other Google tools.

For more information on how to use Google+ for Business, Simply Business has put together a clear step by step guide:

http://www.simplybusiness.co.uk/microsites/googleplus-for-small-businesses/

Whichever social media platform or platforms you use, they must be updated regularly. If you have a presence on more than one platform, you can use tools such as Hootsuite https://hootsuite.com/ to post your messages to all platforms simultaneously. You can also use this tool to schedule messages to go out at specified times.

All of these platforms are currently free to use, but some have paid options for additional services. As the use of social media is rapidly growing, some businesses will employ team members to look after their social media accounts and post on behalf of the business. Remember social media platforms are communication tools and should be used so you can engage and interact with your customers.

How guests book your hotel

How a guest makes a booking with your hotel will have an impact on your bottom line. Earlier I mentioned how important it is to ensure that your website is responsive. This is so potential guests can not only view your website on a mobile device, for example, but they can also book directly with you on such a device. According to Plesman (2015), research carried out by Revinate shows that 63% of travellers will use a mobile device to make a booking.

Hoteliers are now making a much more concerted effort to encourage their guests to book directly with them, with Marriott International, Hilton Worldwide and Starwood offering free Wi-Fi to their loyalty members who used direct channels to make their bookings.

To be honest, most independent hotels are already offering free Wi-Fi to their guests, as this is seen as adding value to their stay. So how else can you encourage more direct bookings and reduce the reliance on using online travel agents? One way is to find out how your guests like to book. Guests like to hear from other guests, and that is one reason why the growth of Airbnb should not be ignored.

Airbnb at first was seen as a threat by many in the hotel industry, although hoteliers can learn from what this company has done to improve their own offering. It is no longer a case of guests using Airbnb to stay in someone's spare room when all the hotels in the local area are full; they can now rent out whole apartments and even castles. According to Hotelsmag.com (2015), boutique hotels are now listing their rooms on Airbnb as they only charge 3% compared to the 10%–25% charges from other online travel agents.

One of the reasons your guests will look at sites such as Airbnb or online travel agents is because they want to find out how your previous guests have rated you. So one site you must have a presence on is TripAdvisor.

Your TripAdvisor reviews

TripAdvisor is the main review site that your potential customers will visit to get a feel for your hotel. TripAdvisor gives you access to powerful business building tools so you can optimise your listing, manage your reviews and track your performance, drive traffic to your website and increase your direct bookings, but what a lot of hoteliers fail to do is actually claim their property on TripAdvisor.

More information on how to do this is available on this link: https://www.tripadvisor.com/Owners

Written reviews have to be taken seriously as once they are published they are in the public domain, and it is your reputation that is being praised or criticised. So what is it about staying in a hotel that will determine whether you get a positive or a negative review? Research using text analytics that has been carried out by the Cornell Centre of Hospitality Research (2016) reports:

One particularly noteworthy finding is that negative reviews tended to be relatively long and they focused tightly on a limited number of hotel attributes. In particular, unhappy guests focused on elements relating to the value provided by the hotel and its transactions, that is, the mechanics of the stay. On the other hand, guests who wrote relatively briefer reviews that took a wider view of their hotel stay generally assigned higher ratings.

One point I always make to my clients in relation to reviews is that, whether positive or negative, all reviews should be responded to as this shows that you are listening to your customers. Murphy (2015) states that from research carried out by Revinate, 84% of users agree that an appropriate management response to a bad review improves the impression of the hotel.

Having read your reviews, your guest will then make an informed decision as to whether or not they will book with you. Once they have decided to make their booking, you want them to book directly with you. TripAdvisor will give a link to your website which will encourage guests to book directly.

Remember that your guest will book directly via your website using a variety of technology. They may use their desktop, laptop or a mobile device. Whichever device they use, your website needs to be fully responsive to be able to ensure the booking transaction is smooth.

According to Bishop (2016), on average small properties spend close to £33,000 per year on online travel agency (OTA) commission fees. By moving just 10% of OTA bookings to direct bookings, you could save close to £6,000 in OTA commission annually.

Online booking sites are still important, though, as they will help to direct bookings to you. TripConnect Instant Booking is an example of how this could work for you. Having looked at your reviews on TripAdvisor, your guest can book directly with your hotel without leaving the TripAdvisor website.

Below are some steps to encourage your guests to book directly with you:

- Rate parity – ensure that the price shown on your website is the same as any other website your property is listed on

- Incentivise direct bookers – on your website, encourage guests to book directly by offering a free upgrade or a complimentary breakfast only available when booking on your website. Ensure this offer is not available with any other website your property is listed on

- Offer multiple payment methods – give the option of credit card payment or PayPal, for example. Have different rates dependant on payment method or lead in time

- Ease of booking – make sure it is easy to check availability of rooms on your website and the booking process is quick and simple to carry out.

Once the above are in place, they will become the start of your guest's journey with you. Remember first impressions are visual, and the first thing guests will see about you and your property is your website. It is not until a lot further along their journey that your guest will meet you face to face.

Exercise – book your own hotel

Imagine you are a guest who would like to book your hotel. Go through this part of the guest journey and do a Google search to see if your hotel comes up. Remember your guest may not know the name of your hotel at this point.

By all means search for your hotel name, in which case your hotel should definitely come up on the first page. If it does not then you will need to relook at your SEO. Also do a Google search on hotel type + destination, for example 'four star hotel in Bath'. Read the reviews on TripAdvisor. From TripAdvisor, click through to your website and see how easy it is to check availability and make a direct booking online.

Now ask yourself these questions:

- Did your hotel come up on the first page from your Google search as an organic listing?

- Did the TripAdvisor reviews you read encourage you to make a booking?

- What did you think about the photos on TripAdvisor?

- Did the link from TripAdvisor to your website work?

- What is the impression of your website?

- How easy was it to make a direct booking on your website?

It is also worth doing this exercise with your hotel's competition. What does their website look like? If there is a hotel that ranks higher than yours, check and see how up to date their website is. Remember, updating your website regularly will help with your organic Google rankings.

What you may find is that the majority of search results on the first page will be paid for adverts and online travel agents. Hotels featured on TripAdvisor will also be highly ranked. You want your hotel to be on the organic search list on the first page – that's when you know your web developer is doing a great job.

RESPONSE – MAKE THE FIRST MOVE

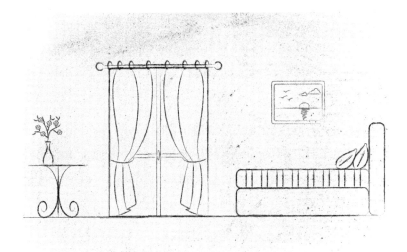

Hotel Booking

The second R is all about your *response*. Here we will look at what happens pre-arrival and how you ensure every guest receives a warm welcome on arrival.

How much do you know about your guest?

Having booked your hotel, your guest will usually receive an email confirmation immediately and then hear nothing from your hotel until they arrive. Remember you want to keep your guest on a memorable journey, so having a lapse in communication can give them the impression you have forgotten about them. Instead, you want them to feel that you are anticipating their stay and making the necessary preparations to ensure it's memorable for them. One way to do this is to utilise the customer data you have available to you about them.

Research carried out by Forrester (2015) on the 'Customer Experience In Hospitality' highlights four key findings when looking at embracing customer data to elevate the guest experience:

- Customer loyalty – less than half of travellers are loyal to a particular brand. Improving the guest experience is the best way to generate some degree of retention

- Seamless experience – guests want a consistent journey when searching for and booking accommodation, and utilising customer data smartly is seen as a key way of enhancing their experience

- Personalisation – travellers want to feel loved when they stay at a property, and therefore hotels need to use customer data to give the personal touch

- Consumer attitudes – guest attitudes towards data have changed to the extent that guests are willing to share some of their personal information in return for a better experience.

Behind the scenes, you and your team should be finding out more about the guest who has just made a booking, and there are several different ways you can do this. Below are some of the ways the hoteliers I interviewed carry out their research on their guests so they can respond appropriately:

Tollman (2015) explains how her reservation team will contact the guest pre-arrival and ask questions to build their profile. They will look to see if the guest has stayed previously and look at any notes on their profile about likes and dislikes.

Munemo (2015) says his team will always find out where their guest is coming from, what brings the guest to their hotel, where the guest has stayed before, then they will educate the guest on their brand in order to manage their expectations.

Thomson (2016) explains how the use of the internet is invaluable, as tools such as LinkedIn can be used to find out more about guests who are due to stay. Information is added to their profile which accurately summarises who the guest is. It will also include any preferences they have, guest amenities they have been given before, and any issues they may have had previously either in a hotel or during the booking process.

By having access to this information on your guest, you can ensure that their stay is personalised. This will make them feel more welcome as you have taken note and acknowledged their preferences.

So having received your booking from your guest, you need to respond to that booking and find out as much as you can about them, whether it be their first time staying with you or they are a regular guest of yours.

Exercise – building your guest profile

Have a look at your reservations and randomly select a guest who has an upcoming stay. Now see if you can fill in all the information below on this guest:

- Full name:

- Date of birth:

- Occupation:

- Reason for staying:

- Flight/travel information:

- Estimated time of arrival:

- Room preferences:

- Special requests:

- Dietary requirements:

- Number of times stayed before:

- Any previous issues:

- Additional notes:

This is the minimal amount of information you should have on guests who are due to arrive, as without it you will not be able to personalise their stay. This information then needs to be utilised and shared among your team, and if there is information you do not have, you can make a courtesy call to the guest.

Personalised experiences engender greater emotional engagement through relevancy – providing customers more of what they want, when they want it.

Hotelier top tip – guest profiles

At the London Edition, General Manager Jurgen Ammerstorfer shared with me how he gathers information for guest profiles and ensures this is shared among the team.

The hotel has a 'black box' which moves from department to department. When one department receives the black box they own it and have to add to it three preferences they have discovered about their guests. This information is entered on to the guest profile, which is accessible by all departments, and the box moves on to the next department.

By working like this, Jurgen Ammerstorfer ensures that his team members are always alert and aware of their guests' needs. Taking note of information by finding out guests' preferences and then sharing it is crucial to be able to create experiences for your guests, and a lot of the time this information is relayed through casual conversation. The more you know, the more you are able to surprise your guests.

An example of how the London Edition team has used information to surprise a guest is when they found out one of their guests was a Manchester United football fan, so they put a Manchester United Football Club scarf on the guest's bed as a gift for them when they arrived.

Your guest's arrival

The day has come that your guest is due to arrive, and this will probably be the first time you will meet your guest face to face. What will you do to ensure that every guest receives a warm welcome?

First impressions are made within three to five seconds by what we see visually. Imagine looking at a photo. How that image has been captured will form an impression on us, and from this build on our expectations.

When a guest approaches your hotel, the first thing they will see is the outside of the building. How this looks will set their expectations.

Exercise – first impressions

Go outside and approach your hotel. As you do so, answer the following questions (as applicable to your property):

- Is signage to the hotel clear and easy to read?

- Are the gardens immaculate and the lawns neatly mown?

- Are the flowers in bloom, shrubberies neat and tidy? (This can also apply to flower boxes)

- Has the exterior of the building been recently swept? (No rubbish or discarded cigarette butts)

- If there is a car park, are the parking spaces clearly indicated?

- Are the windows clean and in good repair? (No rain marks or decaying window frames)

- Is the exterior in good order? (No peeling paint or broken fixings)

- Is it easy to find the entrance?

- What overall impression do you get from the outside of your hotel?

This list is not exhaustive and can be adapted specifically for your hotel, but the reason behind it is to get an idea of the impression the outside of your hotel creates. Does it have 'kerb appeal'? The impression you want is one of cleanliness and high standards – anticipation of what lies ahead when your guest walks through your front door.

What happens next will very much depend on the style of your hotel, although what must happen is that your guest receives a warm welcome as soon as they set foot in your property. To give an example of what I mean by this, below are three very different styles of welcome:

Welcome case study examples
Firmdale Hotels – at the Ham Yard Hotel, as you approach you are greeted by a doorman who holds open the door for you. As soon as you walk into the hotel, the first thing you see is the reception desk. The hotel has been designed like this on purpose so your first point of contact will be the receptionist, and it is the receptionist's role to find out more about you. You will be greeted with a warm, friendly welcome and the receptionist will be quick to engage with you. **London Edition** – when you first walk in, it is not immediately apparent you are in a hotel. The first thing you see is the bar, and to the left is a pool table. It is not until you walk to the middle of the lobby that you see the reception desk towards the far left corner, and as you do this, you

absorb the atmosphere of the hotel and become totally immersed. Again the hotel has been designed like this on purpose because the team wants their guests to feel like they are not in a hotel. These guests are looking for a different experience.

The Halkin by COMO – at this hotel, as you walk in the manager on duty is always available to greet you. The hotel is elegant and discreet, and the welcome you receive is personalised. On arrival you will be presented with a drink of your choice with the hotel's compliments and a refreshing signature scent-infused hand towel to freshen up. For many of the guests who stay here, the manager recognises them automatically and the friendly greeting makes them feel like they are the best of friends.

The way you welcome your guests is key, and that is why it is so important to know who they are so you can welcome them in the appropriate manner. Your goal is to make them feel as relaxed, safe and secure in your hotel as they would feel when entering their own home.

Exercise – greeting your guests

Think about how you greet your guests by answering the following questions:

- What impression does the layout of your lobby/ reception area give to a guest when they enter your property?

- How do you set the ambience?

- Who is the first person a guest will see when they enter your hotel?

- Does your receptionist remain seated behind a computer or are they already standing in anticipation of your guest's arrival?

- Can your receptionist see when a guest arrives? (Depending on the layout of your building, the use of mirrors may help with this if it is an issue)

- Is there a receptionist present?

- Who speaks first?

Having gone through the above exercise, think of how you can improve the way you greet your guests. Remember, whichever method you use to greet your guests needs to be done consistently by all your staff so that every guest receives a warm welcome.

Once your guest is at reception, that's when the check-in process starts. This is the perfect opportunity for your staff to build rapport with your guests.

RAPPORT – SHOW YOU UNDERSTAND YOUR GUEST'S NEEDS

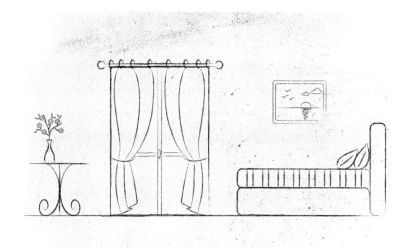

Attention to Detail

The third R is about how you build *Rapport*. Here we will not only look at how you connect with your guests and ways to do this, but will also look at the importance of your service levels and how you can use them to anticipate your guests' needs. Being aware and having heightened attention to detail will be key prompts for you.

Connecting with your guests

Rapport is all about highlighting common interests and establishing a mutual feeling of friendliness. When you meet your guest for the first time, you need to connect with them and form a bond. There are several ways in which you can do this: through your body language, through making conversation and through the words you use.

Connecting through your body language. Your body language will determine how well you are getting on with the person you are communicating with. Have you ever noticed that when two people are in deep conversation, they match each other's body language? They may both be smiling, looking at one another, have their hands in the same position and generally seem relaxed. This is known as matching and mirroring.

When a guest approaches the reception desk they will be standing up, so in order to match the guest's body language, the first thing your receptionist should do is to stand up too. They are then both on the same level which will avoid any awkwardness of a guest having to peer down at your receptionist and it will be easier for your receptionist to make eye contact with your guest.

Making eye contact is key. Some people say that the eyes are the windows of your soul, and they are also the easiest way to read people's emotional state, so it is important to look at your guest when receiving them. Not only is it polite, it shows open communication and gives you an opportunity to notice any distinguishing features about your guest. These could be things to note for future reference.

Top tips for using eye contact

Talking to your guest. It is important to maintain eye contact when talking to your guests, although staring at them should be avoided as this can be uncomfortable for both parties. To combat staring you should break eye contact briefly every five seconds or so by looking to the side as if you are remembering something. If you look down you will break the conversation as this indicates you have finished speaking.

To give you an example, keep your head still and think back to a time when you were at school. As you think back to that memory, you will notice that your eyes move up and to the side. When your guest sees you doing this, they will think you are trying to remember something and will continue to listen to you.

Listening to your guest. When you are listening to your guest it can be off-putting for them if you stare at them too hard. A technique you can use to show you are listening is to focus your attention on one of your guest's eyes for five seconds, then look at their other eye for five seconds and then look at their mouth for five seconds. Keep this rotation going as they speak to you. Using this technique, together with other listening skills such as nodding and occasionally saying 'Yes', shows to your guest that you are listening and are interested in what they are saying. This will keep them talking for longer.

Connecting through making conversation.

The onus is on you and your staff to initiate conversations with your guests, but sometimes this is easier said than done.

One thing that really disappoints me when I approach a reception desk is to find a receptionist working away on her computer, for example, and not acknowledging my presence, and I have to interrupt her to ask a question. We are all busy in our operations, but we need to remember that our guest should be given our full and immediate attention. This means as our guest approaches us, whether this be at the reception desk or elsewhere in the hotel, we should greet them with a courteous 'Good morning' or 'Good afternoon' to start the conversation.

To take this conversation further, we need to ask questions. There is an art to doing this eloquently, which is to use the funnel approach. In order to do this, we need to understand the difference between open and closed questions.

An open question starts with the words who, what, where, when, why and how. By using these words, you ensure your guest responds with a sentence. You do need to be careful with the use of why for an open question, though, as this can seem intrusive. It is better used later in the conversation.

From the guest's answer, you can ask another open question to probe for more information and your guest will give you a more detailed answer. You can then probe once more using an open question to gain specifics and clarification, and it would be at this point that you could use the word why if you felt it appropriate.

To bring the conversation to a close, you could use a closed question to which the guest answers yes or no, or you could give them a specific choice to make.

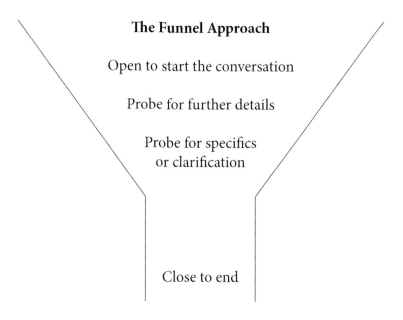

The Funnel Approach

Open to start the conversation

Probe for further details

Probe for specifics
or clarification

Close to end

What tends to happen when we have a conversation is that we use closed questions which end our conversations before they have even begun. It is important to use open questions and the funnel approach as the information that the guest gives can be invaluable.

Exercise – using open questions

Below is a series of typical closed questions your staff may use when interacting with your guests. Rewrite these questions so that they open up the conversation. For example:

Closed: 'Can I help you?'

Open: 'How may I help you?'

Closed: 'Will there by anyone accompanying you?'

Open:

Closed: 'Are you celebrating…?'

Open:

Closed: 'Do you need any information?'

Open:

Closed: 'Will you be staying…?'

Open:

People tend to use closed questions when they are shy or lack confidence. By training your team to use open questions, you will show them as being confident and professional when interacting with your guests.

Earlier we looked at how you can unconsciously match and mirror your guest's body language to help build rapport. Another matching technique is:

Connecting through the words you use. People take information in through their five senses – seeing (visual), hearing (auditory), feeling (kinaesthetic), smelling (olfactory) and tasting (gustatory). Most people tend to rely more on one or two of these senses, and often the language they use will give us clues as to their preferred communication method.

Below are examples of how these communication methods may be used through the use of words:

'I can *picture* what the room *looks* like' – visual.

'I can *hear* what you are *saying*' – hearing.

'I have got a good *gut feeling* about this' – kinaesthetic.

'I can already enjoy the *sweet smell* of your success' – olfactory.

'That leaves a *bitter taste* in my mouth' – gustatory.

When building rapport, you can literally speak the same language as your guest. The table below shows some sensory words and phrases that you may recognise:

Visual	Auditory	Kinaesthetic
See	Hear	Feel
Look	Listen	Touch
Appear	Sound	Grasp
View	Make music	Get hold of
Show	Harmonise	Slip through

Illuminate	Tune in/out	Catch on
Clear	Be all ears	Tap in to
Focus	Rings a bell	Make contact
Imagine	Silence	Throw out
Picture	Resonate	Turn around
Dim view	Overtones	Concrete
Eye to eye	Outspoken	Touch base

People like people who are like them, so by using the same language preference as your guest, you will build rapport with them much quicker.

Exercise – rapport through language use

Imagine you had a guest speaking to you. Work out their sensory preference from what they say and then write down how you would respond matching their use of language.

Example:

Guest: 'It appears the weather forecast was correct for once.'

Preference: visual.

Your response: 'Yes, it is lovely to see the sun shining again.'

Guest: 'What you just said really resonates with me.'

Preference:

Your response:

Guest: 'I am not sure how this contactless payment will catch on.'

Preference:

Your response:

Guest: 'That tasted absolutely divine.'

Preference:

Your response:

By practising these techniques you will be subtly building rapport with your guests in no time at all.

Service levels and standards

Imagine you are going into a store to buy a watch. You may be attracted to a certain watch by the way it looks. You try it on and it feels right for you. You have heard good things about this watch. You decide to make a purchase. The store gift wraps it for you. When you get home you open your package, and every time you wear your new watch it makes you feel special.

Now let's look at what happens when your guest stays with you. They come into your hotel, they like the way the bedroom is decorated, the bed is comfortable to sleep in. They dine in your restaurant and the food is delicious, and the wine complements it perfectly. They check out of your hotel and return home.

They do not have anything tangible that they can take away with them. The only thing they can take away is the memory of their stay, and the only way they will remember their stay is if they had a wonderful experience. That experience has to be created by you for them.

Hoteliers know their products and what they can offer service wise, and they will be building a mountain of information about what their guest expects. They often forget how much information they have on their guest. What they need to do is to be one step ahead of their guest and utilise their service levels to anticipate their guest's needs in order to create this experience.

So how do hoteliers anticipate their guest's needs? Malpass (2016) says this is done 'by knowing the answers to their questions before they even ask me'.

Anticipating guest needs case study examples

At The Halkin by COMO, if a family is staying, the team finds discovering the names and ages of the children is important as they can then tailor bespoke amenities.

A personal card welcoming guests to the hotel creates a little magic. At Firmdale Hotels, ensuring that the welcome note is handwritten, rather than it being pre-printed and signed, adds a more personal touch to the experience.

At Down Hall Hotel, if the team knows that their guest likes to have a gin and tonic at 6pm, the bar staff will know exactly which gin their guest prefers and have the drink made ready for them when they walk through the door.

In order for you to be able to deliver this level of service, communication and training are key. Antonazzo (2015) explains that training employees is needed for consistency. There is no point in having one employee going above and beyond and another sticking to the rules. If you want your employees to shine, you need to empower them so they are free to create these experiences.

Product knowledge is just as important, as Yarney (2015) explains. When he was working at The Shangri La at The Shard, hostesses would be given scripts to learn which gave them the answers to any frequently asked question, so they were always in a position to answer any guest query confidently. On top of this, the service level was elevated by personal touches from the staff that made interactions even more special.

For all of this to work seamlessly, your staff have to communicate with one another. Both Tollman (2015) and Sommer (2016) shared with me that one way in which this can be done is through the front desk staff using earpieces to pass information on discreetly. This is now common practice in the top London hotels.

Imagine you are a guest who has just checked in at reception. During this process you would have given your name to the receptionist. One of the concierge team then carries your luggage and escorts you to your room, and I would expect at this point for them to address you by name during your conversation. The concierge could easily have learnt your name by overhearing it when you checked in or by reading your luggage label – nothing too spectacular about that. But information they could only have received by the receptionist telling them through their earpiece is that you would like your suit pressed ready for an event that night.

When you arrive at your room, the concierge team member

asks which suit you would like to have pressed and ensures it will be delivered back to your room by 6pm as requested. How impressive would that be? You never mentioned this to the concierge team member, so how did they know? How did the receptionist know this information?

This kind of information would be in your guest profile, because the reservation team would have called you prior to arrival and found out that you were staying at the hotel because you were attending a gala dinner that night. During this conversation, you gave the request to have the suit pressed in time for the dinner.

So in order to know what your guest needs before they even know it, you need clear communication between departments and to make use of the information you have about your guest. Little touches will make a big impact.

Be aware, be very aware

The above example can only be carried out if your team has prior knowledge and information about your guest which they can use to their advantage. As you will not personally know every guest who stays with you, it is your role to find this information out.

Through observation, conversation and paying attention to detail, you can pick up on clues your guest will leave as to how to make their stay more memorable. It is down to you and your team to spot these clues and act on them as you see fit.

Being aware case study examples

At The Shangri La at The Shard, Will Yarney shared one story of when a guest left his house keys at the hotel when he checked out. Will had been speaking to the guest earlier, and the guest told him that he was leaving to get the Eurostar. As Will knew this information, he took the keys to St Pancras, managed to catch up with the guest before he boarded the train and handed his keys back. Had Will not been observant and spotted the keys, had he not engaged in conversation with this guest and listened intently, he would not have ended up with a delighted guest who could enjoy a stress free onward journey.

One winter's day in snowy Essex, a car had broken down. Jason Hilton, the owner of De Rougemont Manor, was driving along the road and he pulled over to see if he could be of assistance. The man explained that his wife had not filled the car up and he'd run out of petrol, so Jason gave him a lift to the nearest petrol station. As they were driving, he mentioned he ran the hotel and discovered that the man was a previous guest. Since that encounter, the company that the man works for has become a key account for the hotel.

Warren Miller recalls a time when he was working at The Wellesley and a famous guest stayed with her partner. This guest was an avid Twitter user. On opening the complimentary jar of jelly beans provided by the hotel, she noticed there were no liquorice ones and she tweeted about this. Having seen the tweet, the staff at The Welles-ley went out to Harrods and bought some liquorice jelly beans to put in a jar. When the guest came to check out, these were presented to her as a parting gift, much to her delight.

REFINE – PERSONALISE THEIR EXPERIENCE

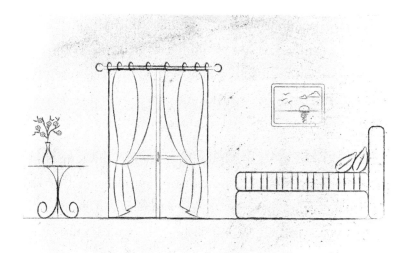

Guest Profiles

The fourth R is all about how to *Refine* your guest's experience; how the use of guest profiles can assist you to personalise a guest's stay. You will be gathering a lot of information about your guest, and how you use this will make your guest's journey a success. Remember, because you want to keep your guest on a long and memorable journey with you, your hotel should not just be a stopping point for them to rest their head.

Let's first look at how to collate this information, which will involve getting a basic understanding of the technology behind the scenes.

Customer relationship management

Customer relationship management (CRM) can be as simple or complex as you would like to make it. At the end of the day, you need somewhere that you can capture your customers' data, ideally all in one place. You also need to think about how you will use this information.

CRM software used to be used purely for sales and marketing purposes, but businesses are now realising that the information they have on their customers can be used in other ways. Crucially, you as an hotelier can use this information to record what your guests like and dislike, and their history with you. Your staff can then use this information to personalise your guests' stay. Some CRM software tools will even link to your customers' social media profiles so you can gain even more information about them.

For a small guesthouse, if you are just looking for a platform where you can collect email addresses and add some information about your guests, and maybe send out emails with promotions, then you might want to look at an email marketing solution such as MailChimp. As with most software these days, you can get the basic version which is often free, but to have access to more features, you would have to subscribe to get a better package.

For larger hotels, you would probably be using a property management system which would have automated emails integrated into it. A word of warning with templated automated emails – you must personalise these. If guests receive a standard email response, they probably won't read it.

Property management systems

A property management system (PMS) in its most basic form is essentially your main computer system that looks after all your room bookings, and you will use this to check your guest in and produce their bills. As time has gone on, these systems have become much more advanced.

Used in isolation, these systems can cause you problems such as overbooking and payment issues. Unless, that is, you choose a more up to date property management system or even upgrade your system. Ideally you want a fully integrated system whereby the various different interfaces, such as your website, online travel agent bookings and point of sales systems, will talk to one another and be compatible.

Integrated systems in The Cloud

There are a whole host of different property management systems out there, and when there is so much choice it is hard to decide on what you need. This will depend on the size of your establishment. Work out what your property needs from the system and how you will make best use of the information that will be generated for you.

> ### Top tips to consider when choosing a property management system
>
> **Affordability.** What is your budget for implementing and using a property management system? Choosing an operator that has a Cloud based system will mean you will not have to buy in specific hardware upfront, and you can even keep an eye on your reservations while you are out and about with your laptop. It may be easier to look for a supplier that has a monthly subscription package to help control your costs.
>
> **Integration.** Booking systems purchased five to ten years ago ran very much in isolation, and now, with web marketing and online distribution channels, you need a fully integrated system. Of today's boutique hotel reservations, 50% come from online. As mentioned earlier, you need to be able to handle direct bookings from your responsive website, as well as from the various online travel agents you will be working with. All of this should link in to your property management system.

Food and beverage integration. For larger properties, food and beverage may be a revenue stream that is integral to your business. You may need to consider the best way of managing restaurant reservations, implementing tableside ordering and capturing dining information which could be used for other promotions and loyalty programmes, for example.

Whatever size your property is, as technology advances you need to be able to find the best software solution for you. Integrated systems will make your life as an hotelier much easier. There are now suppliers who have systems such as Little Hotelier http://www.littlehotelier.com/how-to-choose-an-all-in-one-pms-system-for-small-hotels/ or Eviivo https://eviivo.com/who-uses-eviivo/ that can cater for the small bed and breakfast owner with only a handful of rooms.

If you are unsure as to which property management system you need to use, then you can attend hotel trade shows such as Hotelympia or the Independent Hotel Show in London. There the suppliers will be able to give you a demonstration of how their system works and you can talk through with them what your specific requirements are.

Once you have your system in place, then you need to ensure you utilise it fully. This is something that a lot of hoteliers fail to do, instead only using it for their general day to day operations.

Make use of your guest profiles

One key element that your property management system should have is the option to build and update your guests' profiles – that is information on guests who stay with you. At the beginning of this book, under the section entitled 'Creating A Star Quality Experience', one of the first exercises I asked you to complete was to find out how well you know your guests. Having completed that exercise, you can put the information in the profile for each of your guests and continually update these profiles. The way you use this information will help you to personalise your guests' experience when they stay with you.

When you have a regular guest, this can be quite easily done as you can refer to their profile and remind yourself and your team of how they like their room to be prepared. Do they have a preference for a certain type of pillow? Are there specific flowers they like to have in their room, or flowers that should be avoided? What newspaper do they like to read? Do they like to sit in a specific area of your restaurant when they dine with you? What is their preferred wine?

In the section 'Response – Make The First Move' we looked at building a profile when you have a new guest by finding out more information at the reservation stage, but none of this information is of any use if it is not communicated clearly with the whole of your team. At the start of the day this can be done through team briefings, and as the day goes on, your staff need to be able to access information which needs to be evident in guest profiles.

Sommer (2016) explains that on the property management system used at one of the hotels he has worked at, the staff can grade their guests according to the length of stay and how often they have stayed. The longer the stay, the more attention is given to that particular guest. For example, a regular guest will be met on arrival and given a card from which they can choose a gift item, or a long stay guest may be invited to dinner with the general manager.

At the moment, though, what we are doing is using past information to be prepared for our guest and anticipate what they will expect from us on arrival. Once our guest is with us, the experience has to continue for them, so that is when your staff can really shine as they display random acts of kindness. This is the real secret of how to refine your service and personalise it.

Random acts of kindness

I remember watching a film which came out about fifteen years ago. A young boy had a school project where he had to come up with an idea of how he would change the world. His idea was to *Pay It Forward*, which was the title of the film.

What this meant was that he had to do something out of the kindness of his heart for three total strangers. The recipients of his kindness then had to pay it forward and help another three strangers. These three strangers would pay it forward to another three, and so on. By paying it forward, people ensured these good deeds would soon go viral and the world would become a better place.

The concept of paying it forward lives on, especially in the hospitality industry. These days we speak less about customer service as the emphasis is now on guest experiences. To enhance guest experiences, hotels are always looking at ways to surprise and delight their guests, and the way they do this is by paying it forward through random acts of kindness. Yummy Pubs have taken this a step further – in their boutique pubs with rooms, they have advertised a vacancy for a 'Head of Random Acts of Kindness'.

Being kind and courteous should be a given in the hospitality industry, so holding the door open for a guest, carrying luggage and wishing someone a pleasant stay is all part of the job. The random acts of kindness we are talking about are much grander gestures than these, such as:

- Returning forgotten items to a guest by delivering them personally, for example going to the airport to ensure the guest receives their item before boarding a flight for their onward journey

- Having a fridge outside your restaurant fully stocked with leftover food which the homeless can help themselves to

- Delaying a flight so two of your passengers can

disembark just before take-off because they have received news of a dying relative and want to be at their bedside, then giving them complimentary flight tickets for another time.

While your guests are staying with you, there will always be opportunities for you to pay it forward by delivering random acts of kindness. It is up to you to be observant, aware and listen to your guests, then these opportunities will show themselves. Selfless acts will make you feel good, as well as giving your guest a memorable experience they will treasure. When people experience great things, they love to share it.

Random acts of kindness case studies

Ben Malpass from Belgraves shares a time when he or-ganised a recording session at Abbey Road Studios for a guest who was an up and coming guitarist from Canada. The guest was obsessed with The Beatles and said that experience was the best day of his life.

Matt Mason, owner of The White Hart and Masons, has a regular guest who had a stroke. As Matt's hotel is in quite a remote location, whenever this guest now stays, Matt gets someone from the hotel to pick him up and drop him back to his home afterwards.

General Manager Andrew Oxley from Down Hall Hotel told me of a time when he had an American guest who crashed his car about 20 miles from the hotel. The hotel concierge drove out to him with Andrew and organised for the car breakdown services to pick up the car. The concierge took the guest back to the hotel, and Andrew waited for the pick-up truck to arrive. That was twenty years ago, and every year the hotel still receives a Christ-mas card from this guest.

What random acts of kindness have you shown to your guests? My challenge to you is to pay it forward and deliver random acts of kindness to three of your guests within the next three days. I want you to encourage your staff to do the same, and continue to do so. I also want you and your staff to share these random acts of kindness by joining our 'Hospitality Superheroes' Facebook group https://www.facebook.com/groups/hospitalitysuperheroes/ and posting a thread for your hotel entitled 'Hotel Name – Random Act of Kindness Challenge'. Add a new comment to this post each time you share a random act of kindness you have shown to your guests, and I will then pay it forward by giving the hotel that posts up the most examples…

Well, if I tell you now it won't be a random act of kindness, so you will have to keep an eye out to see which of our hospitality superheroes goes above and beyond.

A little bit more information on this Facebook group: the 'Hospitality Superheroes' group is for all hospitality professionals to join in order to share your knowledge and expertise. If you have a question about anything hospitality related, post it up and our community will be your superhero and come to your rescue. You might work in a hotel or restaurant and have a question around your operations, staffing, promotions or suppliers, for example, or you may be new to the industry and looking for advice on how to get your first role in hospitality. Whatever your position, join our community and become a superhero to your hospitality colleagues. Give the gift of giving – it is contagious.

Top tip

When posting in a Facebook group, every time you add a comment to that specific post, it will get moved to the top. So to stay at the top, keep adding comments to your original post.

If at this point you are asking, 'How can I carry out three random acts of kindness in the next three days?', remember at the start of this book I explained about moments of truth, and how on their journey your guest will have numerous encounters with you and your staff throughout their stay? A moment of truth is an opportunity for you to deliver a random act of kindness. No matter how small or grand the gesture, please do share it.

Random acts of kindness opportunities

Encourage your staff to think out of the box and to do things differently. Turn random acts of kindness into a competition and reward staff for taking the initiative. Think about how to work proactively rather than reactively.

Below are some examples of how you could do this:

Scenario 1: you check the weather and discover that it is going to rain today. Be prepared for this event and have umbrellas readily available for your guests to use. If you have branded umbrellas you have a win-win situation here, as your guests will be advertising your hotel when they use your umbrellas. When a guest returns the umbrella to you, let them keep it as a souvenir. Every time it rains and they use the umbrella, they will remember you.

Scenario 2: your guest is new to your area and asks you to call a taxi to take them to their destination. Ensure you give your guest a business card with your name and the hotel's address and contact number. When they then need to return to your hotel, all they need to do is to show this to the taxi driver taking them back and they will arrive safely at your hotel after their day out.

Scenario 3: you have a conference at your hotel and the presenter's laptop needs specific adaptors for the HDMI cable to connect to the screen provided, which the presenter does not have. Ensure you have spare cables for the various connectors, or alternatively have a spare laptop they could use, together with a spare USB key so they can transfer the information for their presentation. There is nothing more stressful for a presenter than having equipment that does not work on the day. You want to make sure everything is in hand and runs smoothly for them.

Exercise – random acts of kindness

Put together some scenarios of your own that could typically happen in your hotel. Think about what facilities and services you have and how you can make it easier for your guest to access these.

Scenario: _____

_____

_____

_____

_____

Scenario: _____

_____

_____

_____

_____

Scenario: _____

_____

_____

_____

_____

Now give these scenarios to your staff and get them to come up with ways to enhance your guests' experience through random acts of kindness. Each day you could highlight the best example of how your staff have paid it forward.

I am sure there are many other scenarios you can think of, or may have experienced in the past. Think through what could happen and how you can improve the situation for your guests. By thinking on your feet, you and your staff will be delivering random acts of kindness like there is no tomorrow.

REVIEWS – GET YOUR GUEST TO RAVE ABOUT YOU

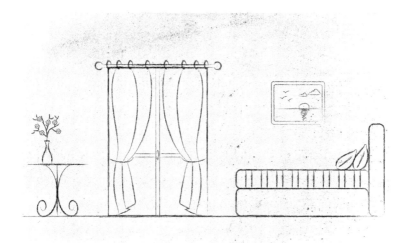

Online Reviews

The fifth R is all about the goodbye and what happens afterwards. You want to get your guest to *Review* their stay with you because you left a lasting impression that they want to share. Whether it be on Facebook, Twitter, Instagram or TripAdvisor, you want there to be constant chatter about your hotel on social media as this is the quickest way to spread news of the wonderful experiences you have been creating for your guests.

A fond farewell

When the time comes for your guest to depart, the way you say goodbye needs to have just as much of an impact as how you welcomed them. The usual scenario is the guest checks out, leaves their key and leaves the building. Then they are left to their own devices.

Check-out time is probably the last time you will get to speak with your guest and you need to take the opportunity to ensure that they leave with a smile on their face. If you have been following the steps so far, you will have built up a good relationship with your guest, so you can afford to take a little more time with the check-out. Rather than rushing them out through the door, find out how their stay has been and if there is anything else you can do for them before they leave. Some hotels will even present their guests with a small parting gift.

Memorable farewell case studies

At Staybridge Suites the reception team is empowered to give a little take home gift to their guests. Depending on who the guests are this might be a mug, a book, a keyring or a postcard – just a little keepsake that will remind them of their time at the hotel.

At The London Edition, one staff member was talking to a guest who commented that he liked specific items in the mini bar which were not available in his country. The staff member then organised for these items to be placed in a 'goodie bag', and when the guest departed this was presented to him to keep him going for his journey home.

To be able to deliver a fond farewell, you need to ensure that the departure process is as smooth and stress free as the guest's arrival.

Top tips to ensure a smooth departure

- Have your guest's bill ready and ensure that it is accurate. There is nothing worse than having accounting queries at the end of the guest's stay as this is the last thing they will remember and they are likely to forget everything you have done for them so far

- Use your guest's name during the check-out process to show recognition and make your service more personal

- Mention something in the conversation about the guest's stay. For example, if they have been shopping, ask if they had a successful shopping trip. You may have noticed bags they have from a certain store and you could mention that

- Ask them about their onward journey and if they need assistance with luggage, a taxi or anything else you can help them with

- Provide the guest with a small parting gift that has been personalised based on what you know about them. Present this in a gift bag which will add to its excitement and intrigue

- Let them know that you look forward to welcoming them back again.

Sharing their experience

Having had a wonderful experience with you, your guest wants to share this with the world. We have already looked at the importance of TripAdvisor in 'Resources – Make It Easy For Your Guests To Find You'. According to Little Hotelier (n/d):

- (Statistic Brain) 49% of travellers won't book a hotel without reviews

- (Statistic Brain) 81% of travellers find user reviews important

- (Edelman) 70% of global consumers say online consumer reviews are the second most trusted form of advertising

- (Trip Barometer) 93% of global travellers say their booking decisions are impacted by online reviews

- (Bright Local Study) 88% of consumers trust online reviews as much as personal recommendations.

How can you encourage your guests to write reviews and share their experience so future guests will benefit too?

Catch them while they are still in-house with you. Ideally you want your guests to be raving about you as and when great things happen. So you could subtly leave them prompts to do this with tent cards in their room saying 'Tell us how your stay is going so far'. Include the social media icons that you have a presence on so they will use these mediums to share.

Comment cards and boxes for some can be a little old fashioned, so if you want to be more up to date you can use a tablet. This tablet will have a short questionnaire which the guest is presented with to capture their feedback before they leave the hotel. Really you only need two questions:

- How was your stay?

- What one thing could we have done to make it even better?

Questionnaires can easily be put together using one of these free platforms:

Survey Monkey https://www.surveymonkey.co.uk/

or Google Forms https://www.google.co.uk/forms/about/

Engage on social media. Ensure that information for your Facebook Page, Twitter, Instagram and Google+ Business Page is easily found so your guests can connect with you online. You need to be watching and listening closely so that you can respond in a timely manner to their posts.

Offer incentives. Do not be shy in asking your guest to post up a review online. You could offer an incentive, for example put them into a prize draw where they could win a complimentary stay.

Use apps. There are various applications, or apps, around now where guests complete a short online questionnaire about their stay. Once they have completed it, they are offered a voucher for a complimentary drink which they can either save for another time or redeem there and then.

The Letyano app https://letyano.com/ is one such feedback solution where the customer downloads the app and has just seven questions to answer. The app can only be accessed for your establishment while the guest is still in the location so the feedback they give is fresh in their mind.

Run competitions. Ask your guests to share their photos on social media, and those who do can be entered into a competition.

Saying thank you

Most hotels now send out a post-stay email. A lot of property management systems will have this as an automated email that is sent out after your guest has stayed with you. You need to make this email personal and engaging so your guest completes your call to action, which will be to write a review. As an added bonus you may want to include a post-stay incentive such as a discount off their next stay.

Top tips for your post-stay email

Ola (2014) gives these top tips of how to get the best out of your post-stay email:

- Write as if you are addressing a friend

- Make it easy to share with direct links to pages on social media

- Keep it personal – make sure your emails are signed by an actual staff member and offer at least two ways to contact that person

- Mention current offers and promotions

- Showcase one of your notable features, such as your fluffy towels

- Ask for feedback and provide a direct link to TripAdvisor

- Reach their friends – offer an incentive for their friends to stay with you.

Below is an example of a personalised email that she received from citizenM hotels, which are known for the way they connect with their guests. It is fun to read and will make a guest want to follow through. Take a look at how they have reinvented their post-stay messages to guests:

Dear citizen Junvi,
(giving the feel of an exclusive club)

Thanks for coming to stay with us, attached is an overview of your stay.

If your own bed now feels a little small compared to the one in your citizen room, I wish to offer our sincere apologies.
(Conjuring up the guest's memory of the hotel room and the experience.)

I'd like you to help us improve your future stays with citizen. If you have a spare minute, please grab a mouse and send us your feedback.
(Asking for feedback immediately and in a fun, authentic way.)

We really hope that you loved your experience so much that you will share it with other citizens by reviewing your stay here on TripAdvisor.
(Directing the more positive reviews to TripAdvisor.)

Alternatively, if you have feedback that needs my immediate attention, you can email me directly at my personal email address.
(Keeping it personal, instead of a generic email.)

Thanks for your time. Until your next stay at citizen, dream of soft pillows and fluffy towels.

Name of General Manager
(a real person)
General Manager
citizen Hotel New York

PS. If you have pictures or would like to share more with fellow citizens, feel free to do it via our Facebook page.
(Keeping guests even more engaged!)

Another way to get feedback is to send a physical thank you card in the post. You give welcome cards on arrival, so why not send thank you cards on departure? A hand written card from you as the manager will definitely make your guest feel special.

RETAIN – KEEP YOUR RELATIONSHIP STRONG

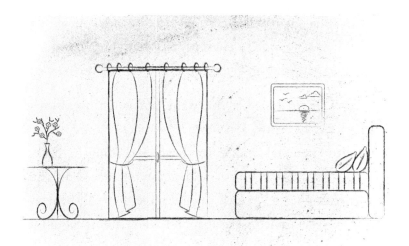

Always in our thoughts

Having gone to all the trouble of looking after your guest, you want to *Retain* them, so this sixth section looks at tips on how to let your guest know you are still thinking about them even though they are not currently staying with you. Remember all that data you collected on your guest when they registered with you? Well now is the time to make use of it.

Birthday greetings and anniversary wishes

When registering to stay at your hotel, your guest would have given you their date of birth. They may have stayed at your hotel to celebrate a special occasion, or perhaps had their wedding reception there. All this information is valuable as you can use it to send your guest a birthday greeting or anniversary wishes. A lot of restaurants do this, together with an email giving their customers a discount voucher or a complimentary bottle of champagne when those customers celebrate a birthday or special occasion at their venue.

Call me old fashioned if you want, but when it comes to celebrations like this, I believe it is much more personal to receive an actual card in the post. According to Tinker (2015), postal marketing is still far more successful than email marketing on return on investment (ROI) when it comes to restaurant marketing, and I am sure it would be the same, if not better, for hotel marketing.

Tinker (2015) specialises in birthday marketing for restaurants in Australia and has done a comparison between email marketing and postal marketing. He gives an example of one of his clients who has 14,032 customers in their database. From this they have 13,248 with physical addresses and 13,932 with dates of birth. This client spent $44,706.31 in birthday card postal marketing, and from this generated $674,740,000 in sales. Once the costs had been deducted, the net contribution from the birthday card campaign was $344,389.69 over two years.

To show how this has been broken down, in one month the client sent out 1,176 cards which cost them $1,716.96. It brought in $24,511.00 in sales, and the net contribution from this was $12,255.25.

The same company did an email campaign to 10,077 customers and the open rate was 38.3%. This meant just over 3,800 customers opened the email, which is a very good open rate, but from this they only got twenty-six redemptions. These customers brought in friends with them, so the total amount of diners was seventy-eight. The total revenue from this promotion was $3,537.00 with a net contribution of $2,171.36, which is very little for a restaurant. So it can be seen that the birthday card postal campaign had a much better take up than the email campaign.

These days, with so many email campaigns being sent out, most of them are never read and are deleted straight away or end up in the spam folder. Everyone likes to receive a card on their birthday or anniversary, and the recipient will open the card so your message and offer will be received.

Exercise – birthday card campaign

Find the answers to the following questions:

How many customers do you have on your database?

How many of these customers do you have a physical address for?

How many of these customers do you also have birth dates for?

This is the total amount of customers you could send out birthday cards to.

If you are using a hotel property management system you should have all this information to hand, and every customer should have a physical address and date of birth entered.

Work out the following for your property:

Number of customers x cost of card and postage = A. Average spend per head - costs = B. Number of guests who take up your offer = C. C x B = potential revenue - A = potential profit from campaign.

Example: 1,000 customers x £1.00 for card and postage = £1,000 to send out birthday cards (A). Average spend per head £100 – costs @ 30% = £70 (B). Let's say only 50% take up the offer (C), so 500 customers (C) x net contribution of £70 (B) = £35,000 potential revenue; £35,000 - £1,000 (A) = £34,000 potential profit from campaign.

I remember staying at a bed and breakfast which sent me a card in the post. I was very impressed by this at the time, although they missed a trick and did not include any incentives for me to book again. They also only sent me the card once, and unfortunately I now can't remember what the bed and breakfast is called. If they had continued to do this every year I am sure I would have returned and recommended them to friends and family. They would even have got a mention in this book!

Touch points

You want to keep your hotel in the minds of your guests even when they are not with you. According to Priestley (2015) it takes seven hours or eleven touch points or four places to gain a pre-sold customer. That is, you need to have made contact with your customers in a variety of different ways before they will do business with you.

The advantage you currently have is that your guest has already stayed with you. Throughout that stay you would have delivered numerous moments of truth, as explained earlier in the 'Creating A Star Quality Experience' section of this book. What you want to do now is to keep your hotel in their mind, so when your guest needs a place to stay again in the future, your hotel will pop into their head as a first point of call.

Below are some ways to keep that memory alive:

Name drop. Follow your followers on social media. When they mention your hotel, you can favourite and share their post. Later on you can mention them or tag them in a post that you create. You could quote a snippet of their feedback and thank them for it.

Special occasions. We have already looked in great detail at the benefits of sending cards in the post. This does not have to be restricted to just birthdays or anniversaries. There are other calendar events you could use this method with too.

Targeted promotions. You do not want to bombard your customers with promotional offers, so you can be selective and only send promotions out to specific customers who you feel would benefit from them. Segment your customers in your database so you can easily select who will receive the different promotions you have on.

VIP invitations. If you are launching a new product – perhaps you have just refurbished some bedrooms – you could send out a VIP invitation to past customers who can attend an exclusive launch party.

Newsletters. To keep your customers up to date with your hotel news, send out regular newsletters. You want to treat your customers as if they are long lost members of your family, so write these newsletters as you would if you were sending a letter home. Share stories, and always add photos.

There is a whole variety of ways to keep your customers

updated. Have you been featured in the news? Have you entered or won awards? What changes have you made to your hotel which will benefit your guests? What are your success stories? How have your staff gone above and beyond? What have your other customers said about you?

You can also link your newsletter to your blog as this will direct your customers back to your website.

Blogs. Your blog should be part of your website and should highlight your expertise. By updating this regularly, you are keeping your website content fresh. Your blog will be read by anyone publically, and people can be alerted every time you submit a new blog post. You can also have a newsletter sign-up link on your blog so you get more subscribers, and you can build up your database this way too.

Exercise – touch point check list

Tick off the items below that you currently do to keep in contact with your previous guests:

- Follow your followers on social media

- Favourite and share guest posts that mention your hotel

- Mention and tag your guests in posts, thanking them for feedback

- Send out birthday cards and/or special occasion cards in the post

- Target your promotions to specific guests

- Send out VIP invitations exclusively to past guests

- Email newsletters to your previous guests highlighting success stories

- Have a link in your newsletter to your blog

- Regularly post up blog entries on your website

- Have a link on your blog for newsletter subscriptions.

If there are any items on the above list that you have not ticked off, then this is your starting point to engage with your previous guests and let them know that you still remember them.

Loyalty programmes

It costs five times more to attract a new customer than to keep an existing one, and your repeat customers will spend 67% more than a new customer. So with this in mind, it is worth looking at how to reward your loyal customers.

A loyalty programme is a rewards programme offered by your hotel to guests who frequently stay with you. Your loyalty programme may give your guest advanced access to promotions, special offers or freebies. Reward your guests for remaining loyal to you.

People love to collect things, and as the saying goes from the old TV game show, 'points means prizes'. Have a look in your wallet or purse now – how many loyalty cards do you have?

According to Colloquy Loyalty Census 2015, in America the average household will hold twenty-nine loyalty cards, although only twelve will be actively used. In 2015, restaurant loyalty membership rose 107% to 55 million.

There are various different ways of putting together a loyalty programme. What you need to bear in mind is you want a system that is easy to administer, your guest understands how it works and they feel they are getting added value by being part of it.

The points system. This is the most common loyalty system, where customers collect points and in exchange are rewarded. However, this can get complicated when you're working out how much money they have to spend in order to be rewarded points, and then how many points they need to exchange for actual rewards. This sort of system is commonly used by fast food outlets where purchases tend to be small and frequent.

The tiered system. This system rewards loyalty through offering small rewards initially, and then as your customer moves up the loyalty ladder the rewards become of a higher value. Tiered systems work well with high commitment, higher price point transactions, such as guests booking hotel stays.

Charging for VIP benefits. Some guests like to feel they are part of an exclusive club and are willing to pay for this privilege. This would be more suited to a hotel that has business travellers who stay frequently. For an upfront annual fee they would be guaranteed certain room types or have exclusive access to a specific lounge, for example.

Forming partnerships to provide all-inclusive offers. Strategic partnerships for customer loyalty can work well for retaining customers and growing your company. This type of programme is normally put together by the larger chains, although it could work for any size company. You need to think what you can provide to your customer that will add value for them. It has to be relevant to them, but will extend beyond what you alone can offer them.

Exercise – loyalty programme

Imagine the loyalty programme example below is being used in your hotel:

Each time a guest stays they are awarded a stamp, showing for example the image of a bed, which they collect. Depending on how many stamps they have, they will be rewarded 'freebies' each time they stay:

- Stay 1 – collect one bed stamp

- Stay 2 – collect one bed stamp – offered complimentary drink during that stay

- Stay 3 – collect one bed stamp

- Stay 4 – collect one bed stamp – offered complimentary breakfast during that stay

- Stay 5 – collect one bed stamp

- Stay 6 – collect one bed stamp – offered complimentary upgrade during that stay.

What system is being used here – points, tier, VIP or partnership?

How would you measure how successful this programme is?

Measuring the effectiveness of your programme. Whichever type of programme you use, or if you just decide to send out special offers and promotions on an ad hoc basis, its effectiveness has to be measured. The most common ways of doing this are:

Customer retention. This will look at how long customers stay with you. Simply put, the customer retention rate is the number of customers you manage to keep with respect to the number you had at the start of your period. This does not count new customers.

There are three pieces of information you need to calculate customer retention:

- Number of customers at the end of a period (E)

- Number of new customers acquired during that period (N)

- Number of customers at the start of that period (S).

We are interested in the number of customers remaining at the end of the period without counting the number of new customers acquired. That means the customers remaining would be E - N. To calculate the percentage, we divide that number by the total number of customers at the start and multiply by 100.

Your customer retention rate = $((E - N) / S) \times 100$

You start the week/month/year/other period you choose

with 200 customers (S). You lose twenty customers, but you gain forty customers (N). At the end of the period you have 220 customers (E).

Now do the maths: E - N = 220 - 40 = 180; 180 / S = 180 / 200 = 0.9; 0.9 x 100 = 90.

Your retention rate for the period is 90%. A good customer retention rate would be above 85%.

According to Reichheld (1996) a 5% increase in customer retention can result in 25%–100% increase in profit for your business.

Net promoter score. The net promoter score or NPS is a measurement on a scale of one to ten which shows the degree your customer is likely to recommend you to others. It is based on the answer to the following question: how likely is it that you would recommend this [hotel] to a friend or colleague?

Respondents are grouped as follows:

Promoters (score 9–10) are loyal enthusiasts who will keep buying and refer others, fuelling growth. **Passives** (score 7–8) are satisfied but unenthusiastic customers who are vulnerable to competitive offerings. **Detractors** (score 0–6) are unhappy customers who can damage your brand and impede growth through negative word-of-mouth.

NPS is calculated by subtracting the percentage of detractors (customers who would not recommend your product) from percentage of promoters (customers who would recommend you). The fewer detractors, the better. Improving your net promoter score is one way to establish benchmarks, measure customer loyalty over time, and calculate the effects of your loyalty programme. A great NPS score is over 70%, and your loyalty programme can help get you there.

Customer effort score. Customer effort score or CES asks customers, 'How much effort did you personally have to put forth to solve a problem with the company?' The answer is ranked on a five point scale from very low effort (1) to very high effort (5), and proves to be an extremely strong predictor of future customer loyalty.

From this, the customer effort score has now evolved into a new statement: '[The organisation] made it easy for me to handle my issue', and customers are asked to express their level of agreement/disagreement with this statement on an enhanced seven degree scale, from strongly disagree (1) to strongly agree (7).

Customer effort score example

To what extent do you agree or disagree with this statement: '[Hotel Name] made it easy for me to handle my issue'?

- Strongly disagree

- Disagree

- Somewhat disagree

- Neither agree nor disagree

- Somewhat agree

- Agree

- Strongly agree.

This score measures actual experience rather than the emotional delight of the customer. Dixon, Freeman and Toman (2000) carried out a Harvard Business Review study and found that 48% of customers who had negative experiences with a company told ten or more people about it. In this way, customer service impacts on both customer acquisition and customer retention.

For loyalty programmes in hotels that address customer service issues, customer effort scores would be a good measure to use. Whichever measurement you use, you do need to measure your promotional efforts to see which are the most effective at retaining your customers and increasing loyalty.

RETURN – WELCOME YOUR GUESTS BACK WITH OPEN ARMS

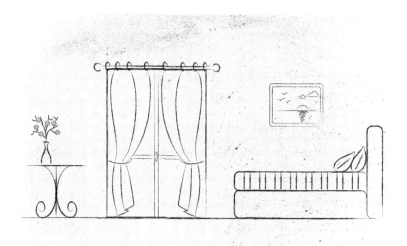

Welcome Back!

The final R is all about what to do when your guest *Returns*. Having kept in touch with your guests and informed them of your news and promotions, you have encouraged them to book with you again for a further stay. Now that you know who your guest is, it will be much easier for you to welcome them back.

Unfortunately, though, this is sometimes where it can all go wrong. Some hoteliers will not acknowledge that they have a returning guest, who is then not recognised or made to feel special. Other hoteliers get complacent with their returning guests, thinking the guests know how they operate so there is nothing else they can do to make the stay special. Remember that your returning guest is likely to spend more on this visit and subsequent visits than first time guests, so you need to keep the magic alive for them.

You have put a lot of effort into the first six Rs – you have great resources so your guests can find information on your hotel and book with you directly. You have responded to them in a timely manner and checked out additional pre-arrival information. You have built a great rapport with them during their first stay with you. You have been able to refine your service to take into account their needs. You have exceeded their expectations and created some memorable experiences. All of this has led to your guests writing some fabulous reviews about your hotel, staff and the service they received. By keeping in touch with them, you have retained them.

Now the last R is to have them return to your hotel so the cycle can start again, and this is when it can be hard in some respects. How do you continue to surprise and delight your guest without it becoming contrived?

The 7 R's to Create Memorable Guest Experiences

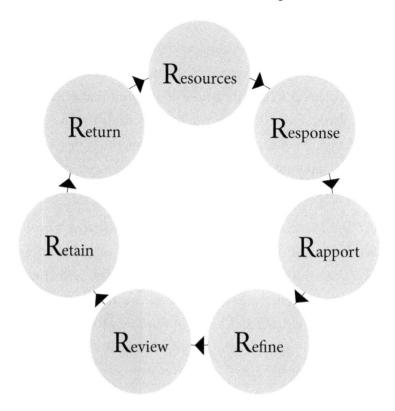

Make a difference

Your guest's return stay has to be as good as, if not better than, their first stay. This is where you really have to make a difference. The advantage you have is a whole host of information on your guest that you will have built up in a detailed guest profile from when they first stayed with you. Now is the time to revisit that and see what little touches you can do that will make a difference to their next stay.

Making the difference – hotelier case study examples

At Red Carnation Hotels, Alex Tollman stresses how important paying attention to detail is. When a guest first stays they are given a fruit platter on arrival, and the housekeeping staff make a note of any fruit that is left on the platter. From this they work out which fruit the guest preferred. The next time the guest stays, the fruit platter is made up only of the fruit the guest had eaten the first time they stayed.

At Ten Manchester Street, Warren Miller shared a time when his staff made a note of the title and author of a book that one of his guests was reading. The next time the guest stayed, the hotel bought the next book that the author had written and left it in the room for the guest. They even ensured it was placed on the side of the bed that the guest slept in.

By being observant and keeping your guests' profiles up to date, you can discover a whole host of things to do to surprise and delight your returning guest. It is usually the little touches that get noticed. You want your guest to think, oh wow, they remembered that about me. Personalising a guest's stay is the key to making them feel special and valued.

Exercise – your return guest
Have a look through your reservations and pick out a guest who has stayed with you before and is returning for a future visit. Now look through their guest profile. Hopefully you will remember who this guest is, so think what you can do to make a difference to their next stay. Add this as a note to their guest profile, so when they arrive, the arrangements can be implemented.

Make your guests feel special

Your regular guests can be as useful to you as you are to them. At times you will be making changes to your hotel, and you will want to know from your guests if they will be happy with the changes you are making, which could be anything from sourcing new toiletries to creating new dishes for your menu. Invite regulars who are staying in your hotel to be your special guests at an exclusive event to get feedback from them on the changes you are planning to make. The fact that their opinion is so important to you will mean a lot to them. They will become your advocates, and if they really like the changes you are making, they will end up promoting them on your behalf by posting on social media. Due to the exclusivity of the event that they have been privy to, they will be dying to tell their friends and family about what you have just revealed to them.

Gaining guest compliments

You should be at the stage now that you know your guest so well that all they can do is to give you and your staff compliments. You go out of your way to assist your guest every way you can, and it is great when this is returned. It is also an excellent motivational tool for your staff.

Some of the best compliments received by the hoteliers I interviewed include:

- Being compared to a crisp white shirt that has just been taken out of its packet. The first time you wear it, it feels good – a great analogy for what the hotel represents to this guest, reflecting its care, service and cleanliness

- Being sent a Christmas card from one of the world's most famous footballers

- Receiving a thank you card from a guest who had to cancel their reservation and change it for another date due to illness. The hotel sent them a get well card and flowers

- Being contacted by a general manager from another hotel offering them a job

- Being told 'You show you care'.

Top tip – guest compliments wall of fame

Have in your staff areas a wall dedicated to guest compliments. Every time a guest compliment is received, whether from a review, a comment card, verbally or from another member of staff, it should be added to your wall of compliments.

This is a great morale booster. Be proud of your accomplishments! It will also give you reminders of what you have done to go above and beyond, and what your guests appreciate about your service.

Just think, in a year's time you could write your own book on the great service stories that your hotel has provided.

As you get to know your guest, you need to be finding different ways of gaining as many compliments from them as possible. This is a much more fun way of operating a hotel than having to deal with guest complaints.

Some unique ways to welcome your guest back

If your guest is an animal lover then there is nothing more welcoming than to be greeted by a friendly dog with a wagging tail. This is what happens at Staybridge Suites in Vauxhall. Waggers, the resident dog, belongs to the hotel manager, and he often comes to the lobby to say hello to the guests.

Staybridge Suites also holds social evenings where guests staying are offered complimentary food and drink and can meet one another and socialise together with Waggers. This is an informal way for staff to get to know the guests better and adds to the personalisation of guests' stays. It creates a great family atmosphere, which makes the guests feel like they belong and are not just some random strangers staying in the property.

Fairmont Hotels and Resorts also have residential dogs, which they call canine ambassadors, at select hotels. For the guest who misses their furry companion or wishes for some additional security, these dogs are available to take on walks and build up relationships with. They even have their own email addresses, and some have Facebook pages!

The Aloft Hotel in North Carolina takes this one step further and guests are greeted by an adorable dog with an 'Adopt Me' vest on. It is believed to be the first hotel in the world where guests can adopt an animal during their stay. The hotel has partnered with Charlie's Angels Animal Rescue and they have one dog at a time at the hotel. In the first six months of the partnership, fourteen dogs were adopted by guests who stayed at the hotel. The dogs are also a great draw to keep guests returning.

Hotels are much more aware now of their guests' needs and what to do to make their hotel a home away from home for their guests. What is important to remember is that once your guest returns, they still need to have the attention they deserve.

WHAT DOES THE FUTURE HOLD?

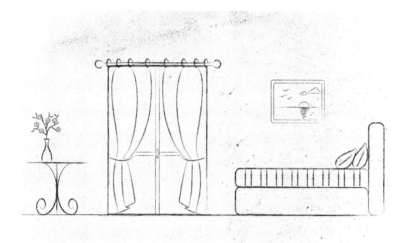

Time to Innovate

From the 7 Rs to creating memorable guest experiences there are two key things that are coming out strongly in order for you to achieve this: the use of technology and the personal touch. Without technology you would not be able to achieve half of what I have shared with you in this book. Hoteliers need to acknowledge that in this day and age technology has its role to play, particularly as guests who have been weaned on it are coming of age.

As technology advances at such a rapid rate, soon the scenario below will be commonplace:

Your guest's flight lands, and as he exits the plane he turns on his mobile. Within minutes his car is waiting to take him to his hotel. It is driverless. Your guest checks his schedule by using TripIt on his mobile phone, and he can view his itinerary without having to search through numerous emails.

On arrival at his hotel, he finds his allocated room number on his mobile through the use of beacon technology. He uses his phone to open the door to his room. No use of key cards here. Through the hotel's mobile app he is able to control the temperature of his room, turn the lights on, close the curtains and order room service. He checks his email on the large smart TV screen in his room. His Facebook page comes up ready for him to post a selfie and check into his location. He then remembers he needs to press his shirt for an event that evening, so the robot butler is summoned and carries this task out for him while he takes a relaxing bath.

Once he has freshened up and is wearing his pressed shirt, he takes a stroll down to the lobby and meets up with his colleagues. They use the co-sharing work space in the lobby to have a meeting before heading out for the evening's event that has been scheduled.

What is missing from this scenario? Service personnel. There was no receptionist in the lobby, no concierge, room service or housekeeping staff in sight. All your guest needed was a smartphone and a helping hand from his butler robot.

This scenario is not as far-fetched as you may think. Driverless cars have been invented. With technological advances, hotels are currently making their rooms as innovative as possible where the guest can control the lighting, temperature and ambience all through the use of a tablet. Mobile phone apps are now so advanced that they can be the key to your room. Robots are now so sophisticated they can cook food, serve drinks and clean rooms.

According to Festa (2016) brands are getting increasing creative with the technology they use. Hilton Worldwide have piloted in-room tablets, although guests prefer to use their own devices for ultimate personalisation and customisation of their travels. Starwood have piloted smart mirrors which enable guests to check the weather, read the headlines and find out the latest sports results while doing their hair. ARIA Resorts and Casinos use in-room tablets as a one touch tool for guests to make wake-up calls, book spa appointments, order room service as well as using them as TV remotes. The use of smart technology is certainly an international affair, and this is a trick that The Peninsula has recognised as their tablets will operate in eleven different languages.

But these technological advances are not just restricted to everyday hotel rooms. The Hotel Astoria in San Sebastian, Spain has the most accessible suite in the world according to Abbadessa (2016). It costs €20,000 to stay there as the room has a special hi-tech lifting machine that hoists the guest up so they can be moved from bed to bathroom. Whatever the guest needs to do, whether it be to open a door, close a window, turn on the television, listen to the radio or answer the phone, can all be done at the touch of a button as it is managed through a tablet.

One of the smartest hotels in the world is reported by Levius (2016) to be The Eccleston Square Hotel, in London's Belgravia. This five star boutique hotel is considered to be the most innovative because:

- Each of the thirty-nine rooms includes all of the hotel's high-tech bells and whistles, including wide-screen 3D televisions and a plush adjustable massage bed

- The Italian-marbled bathrooms are kitted with underfloor heating and a flat screen TV embedded in the mirrors

- Guests can watch 3D movies from the hotel's Blu-ray DVD collection in bed on 46" 3D Neo Plasma Panasonic televisions

- Each room includes an iPad, which doubles as concierge and guest services

- Each hand-made high-end Hastens bed (worth £12,000) has zoned massage controls with electronically adjustable positions

- Bathrooms feature SmartGlass, transforming shower walls and bathroom doors from opaque to crystal clear with the touch of a button

- Nearly every room amenity is controlled by touch sensors, including floor-to-ceiling curtains, lighting, and temperature

- Rooms have the ultimate range of connectivity capabilities, with UK, USA, and EU plug outlets and various ports

- The hotel supplies free-to-use smartphones which provide free international calls and unlimited cellular data

- The hotel's ground-floor media lounge features a massive 103" 3DHD Cinema Screen and provides complimentary Wi-Fi and plentiful ports.

To ensure that guests' needs are personalised, beacon technology is now being introduced. This technology has been around for a while, but the hospitality industry has been slow to catch on. Beacons offer two-way communication so they can be used to gather data on guests' habits, allowing hotels to determine where guests are spending most of their time in the hotel and what peak hours are for the fitness room, pool or hotel bar. They can send messages to the guest at opportune times, such as highlighting a drinks promotion as the guest is walking by the bar.

HOTELSmag (2016) reports that the Corinthia Hotel, St George's Bay has launched the WhatsApp service to communicate directly with their guests. The Malta hotel created a pre-allocated WhatsApp number that guests can use to contact the hotel from anywhere on the island. That is in addition to their 'Twitter By The Pool' service, which allows guests to tweet requests to the hotel without leaving their poolside chair. At present, the guests here are served by the team members of the hotel, although that is not to say that in the future their requests will not be carried out by robots or humanoids. (Humanoids are robots that look very much like humans.)

Where are all your service personnel?

You may have come across the self-check-in kiosks at Premier Inn, although it is not just the budget chains that are becoming more automated. According to Schapp (2016) luxury hotels such as Miami's Faena or 11 Howard in SoHo, New York have given up the hotel front desk altogether, preferring to let guests check in the way they want to through their tablet, mobile phone or via self-service. The Cognizant Travel Survey (2016) shows that travellers want greater automation in hotels with over half wanting to use their mobile device to receive bills (58%), check in (54%), check out (57%), pay for hotel services (51%) and open their hotel room door (50%).

Rather than going fully automated at this stage, Hilton's Research and Development team has developed Connie. Named after the Hilton's founder Conrad Hilton, this 2 foot tall robotic concierge is stationed at the reception desk of the Hilton McLean in Virginia. The robot is connected via Wi-Fi and can balance and stand up. It uses sensors to understand its surroundings, and microphones and speakers enable it to listen and speak, but what is more interesting is the way Connie uses cognitive computing to learn and answer questions about the hotel. A robot that learns from each interaction.

Griffiths (2016) explains how the robot is able to greet guests upon arrival and answer questions about the hotel amenities and services. Through using WayBlazer, IBM's first cognitive travel platform, it is able to suggest local attractions hotel visitors might enjoy. The more guests interact with Connie, the more it learns, adapts and improves its recommendations. While the project is a pilot, it is said to be a step towards using artificial intelligence (AI) robots in customer service roles.

This is not the first time we have heard of robots being used in hotels. At the Aloft Hotel in California, guests who request a toothbrush or razor from the front desk will find Botlr, a short poker-faced servant on wheels, delivering it to their door.

According to Crowe (2015) at the Henn-na Hotel in Japan, humans have been traded in for a diverse set of robots. You can choose to have the English speaking dinosaur check you in or you can opt for the Japanese humanoid with blinking eyelashes. The hotel uses facial recognition to unlock doors as it takes photos of guests when they check in. Porter robots act as automated trolleys. In the bedrooms, concierge robots sit on the bedside and room service is delivered by Muartec, a mobile robot.

Where are the humans at this hotel? They are monitoring the robots through security cameras.

For me, this is taking the use of robots a little too far. There is definitely a place for technology in our ever changing world, but no matter how far advanced robotics and humanoids become, at this point in time what will differentiate your hotel from your competition is how you deliver the personal touch and emotionally engage with your guests.

Remember you want to create a unique experience for each and every one of your guests as you take them on a memorable journey. Hospitality should no longer be about handling guest complaints; it is all about gaining guest compliments. Through random acts of kindness, it is now your turn to pay it forward.

Next steps

You have now come to the end of this book, so what happens next? Well it is over to you to implement what you have read. I know you may have skipped the odd exercise here and there as you went through, so do go back and spend time on these exercises. They are quick to complete and you will gain a lot of insights into how your hotel is currently operating and where you may need assistance to make some tweaks to improve your guest experience.

To make it easier for you to do this, all the exercises are available in a free download at: http://starqualityhospitality. co.uk/book-resource-2/.

Go through this list and tick off the exercises that you have completed:

- How well do you know your guests?

- Moments of truth (MOT)

- Website review

- Book your own hotel

- Building your guest profile

- First impressions

- Greeting your guests

- Using open questions

- Rapport through language use

- Random acts of kindness

- Birthday card campaign

- Touch point checklist

- Loyalty programme

- Your return guest.

If you need further help in implementing what you have read, then please feel free to contact me. You can email me directly on this address: monica@starqualityhospitality. co.uk.

You cannot implement what you have learnt alone. It is really important that you involve your team in this process. Share this book with them so they are clear on the 7 Rs to creating memorable guest journeys. You could even buy them a copy of this book and give it to them as a gift as your way of paying it forward.

Remember to join the Hospitality Superheroes group on Facebook https://www.facebook.com/groupshospitalitysuper heroes/ and take part in the Random Act of Kindness Challenge. I look forward to reading your posts and seeing which hotel is continually surprising and delighting its guests.

I do hope you have enjoyed reading this book and you have found it to be beneficial to you. Whether it was given to you as a gift or you bought it, I have one request to ask of you, and that is to write a short review on Amazon. To encourage you, please do the following:

- Post your review of this book on Amazon

- Send a link or screen shot of your review to info@starqualityhospitality.co.uk.

You will then be sent a free ticket to attend one of my masterclasses or events (depending on where you are and what we have going on at the time).

Now it is over to you to take your guests on a journey they will remember…

REFERENCES AND SOURCES OF INFORMATION

Abbadessa, I (2016). 'World's first five star suite just for people with disabilities'. Available at http://www.west-info.eu/worlds-first-five-star-suite-just-for-people-with-disabilities/

Ammerstorfer, J (2015). Interview with Monica Or, 11 December

Antonazzo, F (2015). Interview with Monica Or, 26 November

BDO (2014). 'Hotel Britain 2015 – The Guide to the Performance of Hotels in the UK'. available at http://www.bdo.co.uk/__data/assets/pdf_file/0007/1327543/BDOHotelBritain2015.pdf

Bishop, J (2016). 'How to Refresh your Direct Booking Strategy – Little Hotelier'. Hotel and Catering Show Hospitality talk, 9 March

Carlzon, J (2001). *Moments of Truth – New Strategies for Today's Customer Driven Economy*, New York: Harper Business

Cognizant (2016). '*Identifying Early Adopters for Emerging Digital Travel Services*'. Available at https://www.cognizant.com/travel-hospitality/travel-hospitality-study

Colloquy (2015). 'U.S. Customer Loyalty Program Membership Top 3 Billion For The First Time, 2015 Colloquy Census Shows'. Available at https://www.colloquy.com/latest-news/2015-colloquy-loyalty-census/

Cornell Centre of Hospitality Research (2016). 'What Guests Really Think Of Your Hotel: Text Analytics Of Online Customer Reviews'. Available at http://www.hotelnewsresource.com/article87872.html

Crowe, S (2015). 'Inside the Hen-na Robot Hotel'. available at http://www.roboticstrends.com/article/inside_the_henn_na_robot_hotel

Dixon M, Freeman K, Toman N (2000). 'Stop Trying To Delight Your Customers'. available at https://hbr.org/2010/07/stop-trying-to-delight-your-customers

Evans, K (2016). Email to Monica Or, 31 May

Eviivo (2016). 'Who Is It For?' Available at https://eviivo.com/who-uses-eviivo/

Facebook (2016). Available at https://www.facebook.com/

Festa, J (2016). 'This Is How In-room Tablets Will Change Your Experience In 2016'. Available at http://www.roadwarriorvoices.com/2016/02/19/this-is-how-in-room-tablets-will-change-your-experience-at-hotels-in-2016/

Forrester Consulting (2016). 'Customer Experience In Hospitality: Embrace Customer Data And Elevate The Guest Experience'. Thought Leadership Paper

Google Forms (2016). Available at https://www.google.co.uk/forms/about/

Google+ (2016). Available at https://plus.google.com/

Griffiths, S (2016). 'Meet "Connie" The Robotic Concierge: Helpful humanoid uses AI to suggest local hotel attractions and dinner choices'. Available at http://www.dailymail.co.uk/sciencetech/article-3483889/Meet-Connie-robotic-concierge-Helpful-humanoid-uses-AI-suggest-local-hotel-attractions-dinner-choices.html#ixzz48vdTTrNK

Hilton, J (2016). Interview with Monica Or, 11 January

Hootsuite (2016). Available at https://hootsuite.com/

HOTELSmag.com (2015). 'Boutiques Listing Rooms On Airbnb'. Available at http://www.hotelsmag.com/Industry/News/Details/63257

HOTELSmag.com (2016). 'Corinthia Hotel Launches WhatsApp For Guests'. Available at http://www.hotelsmag.com/Industry/News/Details/66163

Instagram For Business (2016). Available at https://

business.instagram.com/

Letyano (2016). Available at https://letyano.com/

Levius, T (2016). 'Inside London's Most High-tech Hotel, Complete With Digital Concierge And SmartGlass Walls'. Available at http://www.techinsider.io/inside-eccleston-square-hotel-londons-most-high-tech-hotel-2016-4

Little Hotelier (n/d). *Traveller's Journey To You*. E Book

Little Hotelier (2016). 'How To Choose An All-in-one PMS System For Small Hotels'. Available at http://www.littlehotelier.com/how-to-choose-an-all-in-one-pms-system-for-small-hotels/

Malpass, B (2016). Email to Monica Or, 7 January

Mason, M (2016). Interview with Monica Or, 18 January

Miller, W (2016). Interview with Monica Or, 21 January

Munemo, T (2015). Interview with Monica Or, 13 November

Murphy, C (2015). 'Five Basic Social Media Actions For Hotels'. Available at https://www.revinate.com/blog/2015/03/five-basic-social-media-actions-hotels/

Nibbler (n/d). 'Test Any Website'. Available at http://nibbler.silktide.com/

Ola, J (2014). '8 Ways To Use Your Hotel's Post Stay Emails To Your Advantage'. Available at http://hospitality.

cvent.com/blog/junvi-ola/8-ways-to-use-your-hotels-post-stay-email-to-your-advantage

Oxley, A (2016). Interview with Monica Or, 21 January

Pingdom (2016). 'Pingdom Website Speed Test'. Available at http://tools.pingdom.com/fpt/

Plesman, M (2015). 'Know Your Guest And Own Your Hotel's Future'. World Travel Market Seminar, 4 November

Priestley, D (2015). *Oversubscribed – How To Get People Lining Up To Do Business With You*, West Sussex: John Wiley and Sons Ltd

Reichheld, F (1996). *The Loyalty Effect*, Boston: Baine and Company Inc

Rowledge, A (2015). Interview with Monica Or, 11 November

Schapp (2016). 'Is The Front Desk A Dinosaur?' Available at http://www.hospitalitynet.org/news/4075751.html

Simply Business (n/d). 'The Small Business Guide To Using Twitter'. Available at http://www.simplybusiness.co.uk/microsites/twitter-for-small-businesses/

Simply Business (n/d). 'The Small Business Guide To Google+'. Available at http://www.simplybusiness.co.uk/microsites/googleplus-for-small-businesses/

Sommer, R (2016). Interview with Monica Or, 6 January

Survey Monkey (2016). 'How it Works'. available at https://www.surveymonkey.co.uk/mp/take-a-tour/?ut_source=header

Tinker, H (2015). 'Mail V Electronic Marketing'. available at https://www.youtube.com/watch?v=-oDPmg6y_ZE&feature=youtu.be

Tiny URL (2016). available at http://tinyurl.com/

Thomson, A (2016). Interview with Monica Or, 6 January

Tollman, A (2015). Interview with Monica Or, 3 November

TripAdvisor for Business(2016). available at https://www.tripadvisor.com/Owners

Twitter (2016). available at https://twitter.com/

Visit Britain (2015). 'Guide to Social Media Channels'. available at https://www.visitbritain.org/guide-social-media-channels

Wicks, C (2015). Interview with Monica Or, 3 December

Yarney, W (2015). Interview with Monica Or, 12 November

ACKNOWLEDGEMENTS

I would like to thank the hospitality professionals I have met along the way who have made my customer journeys memorable throughout the years I have been involved in the hospitality industry.

In particular I would like to acknowledge the sharing of experiences and expertise from:

Adam Rowledge – Georgian House Hotel

Alex Tollman – Red Carnation Hotels

Andrew Oxley – Down Hall Hotel

Andrew Thomson – The Halkin by COMO

Ben Malpass – Belgraves

Carrie Wicks – Firmdale Hotels

Francesco Antonazzo – South Place Hotel

Jason Hilton – De Rougemont Manor

Jurgen Ammerstorfer – The London Edition

Matt Mason – The White Hart

Roy Sommer – The Courthouse

Tim Munemo – Staybridge Suites

Warren Miller – Ten Manchester Street

William Yarney – Shangri La At The Shard

I look forward to continuing my customer journey in hospitality and making many more memories.

Finally I would like to thank my publisher Lucy McCarraher and her wonderful team at Rethink Press who have made it possible for me to share my hospitality knowledge with you.

THE AUTHOR

Monica Or MA, FIH, MCIPD

Monica Or is the founder of Star
Quality Hospitality Consultancy
and specialises in working with the
owners/managers of independent
hotels and restaurants to create
memorable guest experiences.

With over twenty-five years' experience in the hospitality
industry, she has worked in and managed four and five star
hotels. She has been involved with the implementation of
standards, hotel openings and refurbishments, and trained
thousands of individuals to develop their people management and customer service skills.

Monica regularly writes for *Hotel Industry* magazine as
their industry expert and has been featured in *The Caterer,*
Hospitality and *Boutique Hotelier* magazines. She has spoken
at hotel conferences in the UK, including The Independent
Hotel Show and The Hotel and Catering Show. She has also
spoken internationally and presented at the COTELCO

Hotelier's conference in Colombia.

Monica runs masterclasses for hospitality students at The Edge Hotel School and Glion Institute of Higher Education among others, as well as for hoteliers and restaurateurs.

As a published author, Monica has been on the authoring team of several hospitality books. Her first book, *Star Quality Hospitality – The Key to a Successful Hospitality Business*, is an Amazon best seller.

Monica's vision is 'to raise the profile of the hospitality industry so whichever hotel a guest chooses to stay in, or whichever restaurant they choose to dine at, they are taken on a unique customer service journey where the hospitality professionals they meet along the way create memorable experiences just for them'.

Monica is available for consultancy, training and international speaking engagements. If you would like to connect with her, she can be contacted as below:

Email: monica@starqualityhospitality.co.uk

Website: http://starqualityhospitality.co.uk/

LinkedIn: https://uk.linkedin.com/in/monicaor

Twitter: @monica__or

Facebook: https://www.facebook.com/StarQualityHospitalityConsultancy/

OTHER PUBLICATIONS

Star Quality Hospitality
– The Key to a Successful Hospitality Business

If you are an independent hotelier or restaurateur wanting to know how to run an even more successful business, this book will take you on a journey of discovery as it:

- Welcomes you into the world of hospitality

- Unlocks the secrets of the business of hospitality

- Explains how customers are your lifeline, focusing on suppliers, staff and guests

- Highlights key industry trends that must be a part of your business strategy

- Shows you how to measure your business success to remain profitable.

Discover the common mistakes made by hospitality owners/

managers, from business structure through to service delivery, and read a host of practical tips and checklists that can be implemented immediately to resolve them. The solutions offered will produce optimum results which will in turn increase your profitability.

This book also comes with a set of free resources that can be adapted and used within your business, based on its checklists and templates. To download these resources use the following link: http://starqualityhospitality.co.uk/book-resource/

If you have already read this book and you found it of use, please do write a short review on Amazon. As mentioned earlier, my offer of a free place on my next masterclass or event applies to this book review also.

To remind you of how to review this book, please do the following:

- Post a short review of this book on Amazon

- Send a link or screen shot of your review to info@starqualityhospitality.co.uk.

You will then be sent a free ticket to attend a masterclass or event (depending on where you are and what we have going on at the time).

Printed in Great Britain
by Amazon

23680014R00091